A Heroic

Life

A HEROIC LIFE

*New Teachings from Jesus
on the Human Journey*

GINA LAKE

Endless Satsang Foundation

www.radicalhappiness.com

ISBN: 978-1508407782

To the One in everyone.

CONTENTS

PREFACE

This is another in a series of books dictated to Gina Lake by the one you have known as Jesus the Christ. I, Jesus, exist in another dimension and am working with the earth and those devoted to me to bring about a much needed transformation of consciousness. The work that I do would not be possible without my connection to all of you who are dedicated to the message of love and peace that I gave two thousand years ago. This connection allows me to have an influence on individuals and the course of earth's evolution.

There have always been those walking the earth who lived in a higher state of consciousness than the rest of humanity. I was but one of them. They came, as I did, to uplift humanity. Many people today are hungry for that upliftment, to be closer to God, closer to their own godhood, their innate goodness. The number of people who are capable of experiencing their divinity in human form is greater than ever before, so those of us guiding the planet feel hopeful that a new paradigm can be established on earth in which every human being is respected, loved, and supported.

This heaven on earth will only be possible through the change of heart that happens when people realize that their own minds have kept them imprisoned in hatred and other negative emotions. This book is written to bring about this realization and activate your divine nature so that you may live together in love and peace and no longer harm each other and the planet.

This is an ambitious goal, and I do not attempt it alone, for there are many like myself in other dimensions and in the body who share it. The gentle woman taking down these words is one of them. Please know that I am with every one of you who puts peace and love above all else. Your reading this book is a statement of your intention for this. Peace!

Jesus, dictated to Gina Lake
April, 2015

∞

Note from the author: To avoid the awkwardness of having to use "hero or heroine," "he or she," and "himself or herself," I have chosen to use "hero" throughout this book and to alternate genders with each chapter.

CHAPTER 1

The World Is a Stage

Every person is living out a destiny, a life that is designed especially for him or her. And everyone has the opportunity to become the hero of his life. What determines this is not intelligence, good looks, luck, or circumstances but a capacity to view life and oneself within one's life a certain way.

How you choose to see yourself and life determines your experience of life and whether or not you become that hero. Your perspective is that important. This book is about a perspective that makes it possible to be the hero of your life. It is also about perspectives that produce the opposite so that you can clearly see which ones do not work and reap only suffering, discontentment, and unhappiness.

The hero has a perspective that works and one that can be cultivated by anyone, and which, in fact, is cultivated by life itself. Life has a way of pointing people to a perspective that brings contentment and peace. That pointing is often accomplished through suffering: When your perspective is incorrect and doesn't match reality, you aren't happy; when it is, you are happy. Life shows you how to live by teaching you through suffering. So ultimately, this book is about how to have a happy and fulfilled life.

Every character in a play has a perspective and a script to follow. If you were in a play, you would immerse yourself in your character's perspective, follow your script, and experience what that character is destined to experience. In real life, you are given a perspective and a script of sorts, but you don't have to stick with it. If you are scripted to play a victim or a perpetrator, for instance, you can choose to play a hero instead. In real life, you can improvise and alter the script as you go. Although you have a certain destiny and a general script, your lives are not actually scripted.

What I mean by destiny is this: You are here for a reason, a purpose. You are here to grow, learn, create, explore life, develop your talents, share your gifts, and learn to love. This is the general curriculum of life, and each person has his or her specific version of it — a more specific destiny. Each of you learns and develops in a way that is unique to you, and that is your specific destiny. Everyone accomplishes this general curriculum at his or her own pace.

You are naturally motivated to develop yourselves, learn, grow, love, create, and join with others. To not do these things would not be human. So you cannot *not* do what you came here to do. You cannot *not* fulfill your general destiny. The only question is whether you will enjoy your life and flourish or go kicking and screaming through it. And why would anyone do the latter? Indeed, it sounds absurd that anyone would resist growing, learning, loving, creating, and developing oneself.

The explanation for this resistance to life is that something else has been built into the human machinery besides these positive drives for learning and expansion: an ego. You could say that the ego is the villain in the human drama, since the ego provides the greatest challenge to human happiness. The ego, which is driven by fear, greed, selfishness, and a sense of never having enough, rails against reality, misperceives life, and thus makes poor choices, which cause the suffering that is the grist for human evolution.

To overcome the trials of the human journey, you, the hero, must clear away the ego's misperceptions, see through its lies, and cultivate your innate resources. Overcoming the challenges presented by the ego develops and strengthens the hero. Eventually, over many lifetimes, the hero gains mastery over the emotions and negative states generated by the ego, and he develops wisdom, discernment, fearlessness, compassion, and kindness, among other positive qualities. The physical challenges of life also accomplish this, but the ego creates necessary *internal* challenges that equally hone the hero's character and make him all that he can be.

In dealing with difficulties, the hero is made strong and is reconnected with his divine nature. Challenges draw forth and develop qualities of character the hero didn't know he had, which are the gifts hidden in the challenge. Life's trials test your (the ego's) false identities, desires, and beliefs and force you to face the ego's fears, which is why the false self cannot survive life's challenges. The ego is the dragon within each of you, which is eventually conquered through life's trials.

The hero's journey — this human life — is a search for and discovery of the greatest treasure of all: the gifts of your true nature. These gifts are your birthright, but they have been hidden from you, kept from you by the ego. These gifts are the wisdom, love, peace, courage, strength, and joy that reside at your core.

The *ego,* as I am using the word, is the programmed aspect of the human being that causes you to feel separate, fearful, lacking, and at odds and in competition with life and others. The ego is a sense of self that feels small, limited, afraid, and combative. The ego is who you are programmed to believe you are, and it is represented by the stream of thoughts that flows through your mind on a nearly continual basis. This thought-stream is primarily about yourself or about others in relation to you.

You need a sense of self to function in the world as an individual, and for that, you can be grateful to the ego. However, you don't need the stream of thoughts about yourself, nor the ego's negative and limiting definitions of yourself, nor its opposition to the way things are.

Contrary to the ego's perceptions, life is *not* supposed to be different than the way it is. You are *not* lacking anything you need to be happy. You do *not* need to be afraid of life. Life does *not* have to be a struggle. Life is *not* a competition. Life is *not* about getting more things and more power. You are *not* actually separate from others or from life, although it does seem that way. The ego's perspective does not reflect reality, which is why it causes suffering.

Believing things that aren't true gets you into trouble, doesn't it? It is easy enough to see this: If you believe a map that is incorrect, you'll get lost. Or if you believe your brother is out to get you when he isn't, that will cause problems between you. Any actions you take in relation to him will be ill-informed and inappropriate. To function well, to survive, and especially to thrive, you need accurate information about reality. But you won't get that from the ego. It has its own perspective and agenda, which is often self-defeating and counter to your happiness.

The ego belongs to the conditioned self, which includes, as the name implies, various kinds of programming and conditioning. Some of this is helpful and true and some is not. Your programming and conditioning is intended to help you function and survive, and some of it does, but some of it does the opposite! What a dilemma. Did you know that your software is significantly flawed? That is part of the problem.

Most people don't know that the software running them is flawed. They don't realize that their ego's map of reality is incorrect and therefore the cause of foolish and hurtful actions and poor solutions. If people questioned this stream of thoughts, this would become apparent, but people don't usually question their thoughts.

People also often don't question the information they have acquired along the way from seemingly reliable sources, such as parents, teachers, and other authorities, much of which is also untrue, unhelpful, outdated, or irrelevant. These mistaken ideas and untrue and negative beliefs, which have become part of your programming, now seem absolutely and unquestionably true. People are programmed to believe things about themselves, others, and life that simply aren't true. So, in addition to a maladaptive ego, misinformation, which is another very poor map of reality, is also part of the conditioned self and, consequently, the thought-stream.

Misinformation and mistaken and limiting beliefs make up the greater part of the conditioning that shows up in the thought-stream. This conditioning, along with many unconscious beliefs, was shaped by people you have encountered and your family, culture, religion, environment, gender, and genetic inheritance, including your appearance, intelligence, health, and personality. This conditioning is the script you have been given, and it largely determines how you will behave—unless the script is examined and questioned.

Such an examination wouldn't even be necessary if people's egos and conditioning provided an excellent and accurate map of reality and of how to be happy. However, most people aren't happy. Most people suffer a great deal and find life very difficult to accept and navigate because of their egos and conditioning.

As a result, the script—the thought-stream—needs to be questioned, or one's story might not have a happy ending. The character might not fulfill his or her specific destiny or even the general destiny of growth, love, learning, creativity, discovery, and expansion to its fullest.

If you have an ego (which you do), then you have been given a script that doesn't lead to happiness. So even if you had the most ideal parents and upbringing, you will still need to learn how to be happy, simply because you have an ego that is resistant to and fearful of life and has an incorrect map to happiness. It's a good thing that you are not the ego (you just *have* one) but something much greater and more mysterious.

The conditioned self, which includes the ego, is the character you are playing. This character will either follow the script or become the hero of his life despite the script. Everyone has a latent hero, just waiting to be brought to the surface and developed. In most people's lives, most of the time, the ego is in the forefront and running the conditioned self's life. But the hero can step into those shoes and become the main actor.

The hero is the reflection of your true self as it manifests through the character you are playing, while the ego is an imposter, a poor stand-in. The ego pretends to be who you are, but it can never live up to your potential greatness because it has a negative and untrue perspective of life.

The inner hero is brought to life by becoming aware of it and by nourishing its positive qualities with your attention. You become the hero by:

❖ Seeing the truth about reality,

❖ Seeing life as an adventure,

❖ Loving life just as it is,

❖ Maintaining a positive outlook,

❖ Being courageous, not fearful,

❖ Welcoming challenges for the opportunities for growth they provide,

❖ Being willing to make mistakes and learn from them,

❖ Being willing to investigate and heal any limiting beliefs, negativity, or untruth within you,

❖ Mastering your negative emotions and lower drives,

❖ Being willing to follow your Heart.

This is how the true self lives as the character you are playing. It is how you can become the hero of your life rather than the victim of your conditioning. The chapters that follow will describe how to cultivate the traits above, which make for a happy life. But first, let's examine the perspective the hero will need for the adventure of life.

CHAPTER 2

The Hero's Perspective

The hero sees life as it actually is and accepts life as it is. The hero knows the truth about life. And what is the truth? How does one discover the truth, and how would you know it if you found it? These are all questions the hero naturally seeks answers to and ones that will be answered in these pages.

The hero's journey is largely about discovering what life is all about, what is true about life. For this, the hero must be an adventurer, a seeker of the truth. She must be willing to discover whatever might be discovered, even if that isn't what she would like to discover. The search for the truth requires courage and fearlessness. Fortunately, what this search uncovers is very good news, although not necessarily for the ego.

The hero is a lover of the truth and, as a result of the search, has discovered that life is good. So the hero trusts life. How did the hero come to be able to embrace life so? Quite simply, she was willing to learn from her mistakes and from the suffering caused by not accepting life as it is, and she was willing to find out the truth.

A desire and willingness to discover the truth about life, about reality, is essential in becoming the hero of your life. Without this, you won't investigate, examine, ask questions, or confront what is false. You will accept the script you have been given and play the role that script defines. You will complain, blame, feel sorry for yourself, be angry, feel afraid and powerless, and cope with all of these feelings badly, primarily through addictive behaviors. You will suffer, and your relationships will suffer.

Not questioning one's thoughts leads to a life like most people are living. Most people don't take responsibility for their feelings because they don't realize that their thoughts — their ego's perspective — created those feelings. They are angry at other people for how they feel and at God for life being the way it is. But what is really to blame is the faulty map of reality they have been given.

Most people are looking out at life through the wrong lens, through their ego's eyes. They don't know reality because they aren't seeing reality, only their mistaken perceptions about it:

While the ego sees problems, the hero sees possibilities;

While the ego desires, the hero is content and grateful;

While the ego experiences failure, the hero succeeds at learning;

While the ego is lonely, the hero is always in love;

While the ego feels lacking, the hero feels complete;

While the ego gives up, the hero perseveres;

While the ego clings, the hero lets go;

While the ego tells a story, the hero stays present;

While the ego experiences frustration, the hero experiences perfect timing;

While the ego is fearful, the hero is courageous.

How can there be two such different perceptions of reality? Since there is only one reality, one of these perspectives must be true and one must be false. If even just one person can experience life as the hero does, that has to call into question the ego's perceptions of reality. When it comes to reality, the majority doesn't rule.

The hero has a correct map of reality because she has studied reality and adjusted the map accordingly. She observes, examines, and questions her thoughts and learns from her experiences. She doesn't accept a thought just because her mind or someone else's believes it. The hero is like a visitor in a strange land, where the customs are unknown. Nothing is taken for granted. She asks: "Why do they do things this way? Why do they believe this? Is that true? What is the result of believing that? Is that the result I want?"

The biggest difference between those who follow their scripts and those who become the hero is that the hero has curiosity. The hero questions and adjusts her beliefs according to what she discovers. As more about reality is discovered, the map is redrawn. She is also interested in learning what other lovers of truth have discovered. She keeps an open mind.

Although there is some truth in the ego's map of reality, so much of its map is distorted by mistaken beliefs: "He shouldn't have died." "She always does that." "I will never get over this." "I can't forgive him." "I'll never be successful." "I can't do anything right." Everyone has thoughts such as these because everyone has an ego. They are the stories the ego tells, which bear little resemblance to reality. They are the distorted map the ego lives by.

The truth is:

He *should* have died (who's to say that death shouldn't have happened?).

She *doesn't* always do that.

You *will* get over this (if you stop telling yourself you won't).

You *can* forgive him (if you choose to).

You can't be anything but successful (from your soul's perspective).

You do many things right.

We can go even farther and say that there is no such thing as "success" or "right." These are concepts invented by the mind, having no objective reality. You *imagine* what success is and what right is. You, your ego, makes it up. Furthermore, what your mind makes up exists only in *your* mind—and that keeps changing! The ego's map is not even based on solid ground as much as shifting sand.

We could even say that nothing that's put into words is absolutely true. Words are a very poor representation of reality because reality is just too mysterious and complex to put into words. People, as well, are too mysterious and complex for words. Words, especially the ego's stories, always leave something out. As a result, the thoughts that flow through your mind aren't as useful as you might think. They contain only a smattering of truth and are therefore a very poor map for how to live your life.

The hero knows this. The hero is guided by something other than the thought-stream—by another stream, which many have called the flow. The flow is reality; it is what is actually happening here and now. It isn't something that is happening in someone's imagination or something that happened long ago or something that will happen in the future.

The hero pays attention to what is real and responds. "What am I moved to do now? What is true in this moment? What am I moved to say now, if anything?" The hero isn't conscious of these questions and doesn't think about them but responds naturally and spontaneously to what is being experienced *now*—without the influence of the thought-stream. Some cognition might be required in a particular moment, but cognition, which stems from the rational part of the mind, is very different from the ego's thought-stream.

In the now, there are no problems because there is no thought of a problem. "Problem" is just one more concept created by the ego. There are no comparisons needed, except maybe apples to apples when buying apples. There is no failure or success, no beautiful or ugly, no good or bad, no smart or dumb, and no better or worse, because these are all concepts—imaginations. They belong to the ego's world.

You may not think of it as the ego's world because it's the world most everyone lives in, since everyone has software that perceives reality similarly. But that doesn't make the ego's perceptions true! Hundreds of thousands of people might agree that God is vengeful or that certain races are inferior, but their agreement doesn't make this so. People have collectively bought into many, many lies because they have believed this thought-stream, and it's time to see this now. It's time to end the madness on this planet: war, violence, hatred, poverty, and the destruction of the environment.

I'm not suggesting you do away with all language, because language is necessary for society. Language makes joining with others possible just as much as it separates. I am suggesting you can be free of the false assumptions embedded in language, particularly language that reflects the ego's perspective, once you see that these assumptions are false.

False assumptions, such as "He shouldn't have died" and "I'll never get over this," keep people in bondage to negative emotions and prevent them from being as happy, fulfilled, loving, and peaceful as they can be. False assumptions turn people into victims or bullies and keep them from realizing their inner hero. On the other hand, seeing through the ego's false assumptions changes everything. Freedom lies in seeing the truth about your thoughts.

Any number of stories could be told about any person, experience, or event and about yourself, and none of them would be completely true. The mind chooses to tell particular kinds of stories, usually ones that make you or someone else right or wrong, or better than or less than.

For instance, if someone loses her car keys, her mind might say: "How could you lose your keys? That was so stupid! You always lose things. You should be more careful. You'll never learn. Dad used to lose his keys all the time. What if I can't find them? How much will it cost to replace them? How will I get to my appointment?" Like so many thought-streams, this example is a combination of stories and thoughts about the past and future. Are any of these thoughts necessary? Do they accomplish anything?

When you take a good look at what goes through your mind, you will find the thought-stream lacking in useful content. Not only are the mind's stories useless and untrue (you are *not* always stupid, you do *not* always lose things, and you *do* learn), but they make you feel bad, and feeling bad is a less effective state than feeling good.

Negative emotions release chemicals in the body that diminish the functioning of the rational part of the brain, making problem solving more difficult. The thought-stream actually undermines intelligent action. You may think this stream of thoughts is how things get done and problems get solved, but it is actually a hindrance. Seeing this is recognizing a very important truth.

Even the more positive and neutral stories in the thought-stream are not necessary or useful, although they're easier to live with: "The sky is unusually blue today. I'm so glad I found my keys. I found them really quickly. I'm happy today." As nice as these thoughts might be, what good are they? All they do is keep you involved in the thought-stream instead of in the here and now. Moreover, positive thoughts, as much as negative ones, maintain the "I" reflected in the thought-stream, the false self. So in that sense, positive thoughts about "I," no matter how true, are not actually so positive.

The exception to this is when you purposefully create a positive statement to counteract a negative thought. Devising a positive, truer story can be very useful in canceling a negative one. However, if you didn't believe a negative story to begin with, you wouldn't need to create a positive one.

The hero finds a positive story to tell or moves through life without a need to tell stories. Most people need positive stories before they get beyond stories altogether. Positive stories can be a bridge from the ego's mistaken perceptions to the truth. What I mean by a positive story is either a simple statement of truth, such as "I can't find my keys," or a story that reflects a bigger and therefore truer perspective, such as "Keys get lost sometimes."

The difference between a negative story and a positive one is how it makes you feel. You know you have found a positive and true story when you no longer feel tense, upset, or unhappy. A positive and true story brings relaxation and peace. If a positive story isn't true, however, it won't bring peace. Pumping up the ego with a positive story that isn't true, such as "I never make a mistake," will only cause more inner agitation.

A lie can never bring relaxation and peace because it isn't meant to. Life rewards you with peace when you believe the truth or tell the truth. When you don't do that, you will experience upset, agitation, and a sense of contraction in your body. Life points you to the truth this way.

In our example, another positive story might be: "My keys must be somewhere." That's the truth and a much more helpful story than the ones usually found in the thought-stream. That story gives you confidence that you'll find your keys and inspires you to look for them, making it more likely that you *will* find them. Instead of wasting energy punishing or shaming yourself, you'll get to work playing detective. Discovering what happened to your keys can even be interesting and fun. With this positive perspective, you'll be focused and involved with all your senses as you explore your environment, not lost in thoughts about yourself.

The hero finds a way to see, or frame, experiences that allows her to stay present, focused, and alert to what is true instead of lost in what isn't true: the thought-stream. The ego tells a negative story, while the hero tells a true story, one that sticks to the truth and doesn't sap her energy or confidence: "Keys are lost for the moment. Time to look for them." This story is not only true, but rational and free of emotional charge.

Does living without involvement in the thought-stream sound dry, unfeeling, and therefore unappealing? If that's your reaction, you might be addicted to the mind's drama. People are attached to their familiar stories, and on some level, they enjoy the drama of being stirred up emotionally, even though that doesn't feel good and isn't productive. Humans have a very irrational side, which is reflected in the thought-stream. This thought-stream is driven not only by the ego, but by the unconscious mind.

There is another reason why people are attached to certain thoughts: They are attached to the images of themselves that the thoughts describe, even if those self-images are negative. They are attached to seeing themselves as clumsy, weak, a victim, unworthy, unlovable, or "less than" in some other way. Everyone has many self-images, many of which are limiting and keep them stuck in negative feelings.

But why this attachment to self-images, even to negative ones? This attachment is part of the programming that is designed to uphold the illusion of the false self. Self-images, especially negative ones, define the false self and keep it alive. They are the clothing the false self wears. Without this clothing, the false self would not exist, so your ego has no motivation to be rid of negative self-images, even if you do.

The ego's job is to create and maintain the false self through self-images. It accomplishes this by telling stories. If you have a self-image of being someone who messes up, then losing your keys is a perfect opportunity to reinforce that image and remind you, through the thought-stream, of just how inadequate you are. You lost your keys—more proof of your inadequacy!

In this way, every little mistake becomes an opportunity to reinforce the negative self-image, when the reality is that mistakes just happen in life—to everyone. Keys get lost. This is just another fact of life, not proof of your unworthiness. Losing your keys doesn't *mean* anything about you.

The ego creates a sense of self by making events personal. Events are just events, but the ego makes them all about *you*: "You lost your keys! How stupid of you!" This is how the ego creates and maintains a sense of being you. But this is a false, limited sense of yourself, not the true you.

The false self is the *you* that suffers and struggles. The true self doesn't struggle but rests in peace, contentment, and awe of life and moves as needed. The hero sees the truth about the false self and cultivates the qualities of the true self.

The hero knows the difference between a story and the truth, a self-image and reality. A self-image may be clumsy, stupid, unattractive, bad, bitchy, selfish, or any other adjective you can come up with, but *you* can never be any of those things. Each of those words is a story about an image of you, not you. You are a most magnificent creation that cannot be captured in words. You can call that a positive story if you like, but it is very close to the truth.

The hero has a way of seeing herself and seeing life that allows her to embrace life as the adventure that it is. She is exuberant, enthusiastic, courageous, interested, fascinated, curious, optimistic, and confident because she doesn't entertain any ideas that would interfere with that natural *joie de vivre*. She sees life as an exciting exploration and a gift. And so it is. The hero sees life as it truly is and rejoices in it.

The only way this attitude is possible is if the hero remains present to life as it is showing up moment by moment and not lost in the thought-stream, which generally results in unhappiness, stress, and negativity. The hero's positive perspective is a function of how present she is in the moment. She knows that being in the moment aligns her with the qualities of her true nature, while being lost in the thought-stream ensures that she will merge with the ego and lose access to the qualities of the hero.

The hero isn't afraid of or discouraged by life's challenges but accepts them as part of the adventure. Without challenges, there would be no adventure, nothing to test your metal against, nothing to stretch you or cause you to grow, learn, and expand yourself—and what would be the fun in that?

You are meant to be adventurers and to expand and deepen yourselves through these adventures. The part of you that loves the challenges of life is the hero. When you are aligned with this inner hero, you say yes even to life's difficulties and find the strength within to deal successfully with those challenges.

When you are able to see life as the adventure that it is, you can face the unknown with courage and gratitude, which are qualities that can only come from one's true nature. The ego knows nothing of either. The ego's perspective of life doesn't help you cope with life but undermines your inherent strength, which is waiting to be tapped. There is a hidden superman or woman in each of you that must be brought to life. It is there within everyone. It is your true self—the *real* you.

The transition from ordinary human to superhuman is accomplished, not by a change of clothes, but by a change of perspective. How surprising! A change of beliefs—to ones that match reality—makes that transformation possible. Change your beliefs, and you will be transformed, and so will your life. As your perspective shifts away from the ego's, you become happier because you gain access to the attitudes and qualities that allow you to love life and cope with its challenges successfully.

You are powerful. That power is unleashed by your capacity to choose what to believe and how to see things. The magical power you have been endowed with is simply the power to choose which thoughts to believe.

The ego has one set of thoughts, while the hero's mind is very different. The hero's mind is emptied of most, if not all, of the ego's thoughts, and those that remain are powerless to get the hero's attention. In their place are only a few neutral or functional thoughts.

In the silence between those few thoughts are found all the qualities of your true nature: courage, perseverance, patience, kindness, compassion, love, peace, and wisdom. Your inner strength—the hero—is found in the space in between your thoughts!

CHAPTER 3

False Assumptions

Several insidious assumptions underlie the ego's perspective, which veil the truth about life and cause much of the suffering inherent in the human condition. We are going to examine some of the assumptions that hold the ego's map of reality in place. Hopefully, this will make adopting a truer map much easier.

Two small words are responsible for a lot of human suffering: *could* and *should*. Let's first take a look at one of these little words that has so much power: *could*. Of course you need this word to communicate, and in many instances, it is useful: You *could* do or say any number of things. Anything, really, could be possible in the future. And it's useful to see this. It allows you to be open to many possibilities.

The problem with *could* is not in its pointing to future possibilities, but when people use it in speaking about the past: "It could have been different." This is always a lie and the cause of a great deal of unnecessary regret, sadness, anger, guilt, and shame. So let's examine this.

Could the past have been different if you or something else had been different? In that previous moment, you could only have been exactly as you were, just as in this moment you can only be exactly as you are right now. The same is true of every other aspect of that previous moment: It could only have been exactly as it was. A precise set of circumstances, conditioning, and choices, too numerous to comprehend, led up to that moment and made it what it was. Many elements beyond your control or anyone else's would have had to have been different for that moment to have been different.

Could the past have been different? That's a useless hypothetical question. What happened in the past was what it was, and no amount of speculation can change that. This rumination about reality is just the mind's way of not accepting a former *now* and its way of taking you out of the current *now*.

Could isn't applicable to the past, and it hurts to think about the past this way. The reason it hurts is because that is life's way of telling you that you are believing a lie. Lies hurt.

The ego doesn't accept much of what happened in the past any more than it accepts what is happening now. However, the only means the ego has to try to change the past is thoughts, so it thinks about the past: "What if...?" "If only...." "I should have...." "I wish...." But these thoughts are powerless to change the past. All they do is make you miserable.

The problem with the ego is this very lack of acceptance. It resists life unless life happens to be showing up in a way that pleases the ego, which does sometimes occur. But mostly, life happens without regard for the ego's preferences. There is life as it is—reality—and life as your ego would like it to be: fantasy. The ego lives in a world of "could be," "should be," and "might be," a world divorced from reality, while life is what it is. Anything except what is actually happening now is just a thought about reality, not reality.

What was said about *could* is also true about *should*. "Life should be different! The past should have been different!" Who says? The ego does, and if you believe this, you'll suffer. This thought, "life should be different," is not a basic truth, but the ego's demand for an ideal world that doesn't exist and never will. This declaration is just a thought in the thought-stream, the ego railing against reality.

Where does this thought-stream come from? Does it speak the truth? Where does the truth about life reside? These are questions you have to answer for yourself. The hero is willing to explore and find out what is *really* true. If the truth lies in the thought-stream, then the thought-stream should be trustworthy. But is it? How true is it really? If it is only sometimes true, you have a problem. Then how do you determine what is true and what isn't? What is truth anyway?

Isn't truth something that can actually be known, not something that is simply assumed to be true? When you define truth as what is actually known, then not that much is true. What can be known for certain is generally what is true according to your current sensory experience without the mind's interpretation or spin.

In a particular moment, for instance, it may be true that the sky is blue. But to say much more than that about the sky in that moment is more like a story, a spin given to this simple fact. The thought-stream might offer the following: "The sky isn't as blue as usual. The sky is bluer in fall than spring. The sky is prettier when it's bluer. The sky isn't blue often enough."

None of these statements the mind might come up with is absolutely true, and some are just opinions. Statements in the thought-stream, such as these, often pass as facts, as the truth. However, the truth is much simpler: The sky is blue — period. As for past events, something either happened or it didn't; there is no *could* or *should* about it. *Coulds* and *shoulds* relating to a past event can never be true.

When *should* shows up in the thought-stream, it indicates a desire for reality to be different than it is: "Life shouldn't be so hard. He shouldn't have said that. I should be thinner." The truth is, wanting life to be different has nothing to do with reality and has little influence on it, except that wanting causes discontentment, and then that becomes your experience of reality. Wanting anything other than what is showing up in reality spoils the moment, which is all anyone ever has. If you cling to the ego's ideas about what it wants life to be, rather than accept life as it is, you'll be unhappy.

The word "should" signals a false assumption, so it is an important word in the thought-stream to become aware of if you want to be free from suffering and live in reality. There isn't a single statement with that word in it that is true or useful. If you want to suffer, then hang on to your *shoulds*. If you find yourself thinking a thought with *should* in it, don't believe it.

Should is a direct rejection of reality. It's like saying no to what is: "No, it should be this way instead. No, he should be this way instead. No, I should be this way instead." Instead of what? Instead of the way it is, he is, I am — instead of the way things really are.

Because the ego wants things to be different, it pretends they can be. But they can't. If an airplane is flying overhead, could that be different? Does saying it *should* be different change anything? It's too late for that moment to be any different than it is. The *now* has already moved on, and the airplane is no longer overhead. Could the airplane be overhead *now* or *should* it be? Why bother with thoughts like these? You can even suffer over airplanes coming and going if you choose to.

Believing a *could* or a *should* is a choice, and that choice leads to suffering. Once you know this, if you don't want to be unhappy, there is only one choice to make. Suffering is something you can do something about. If you believe the thought-stream, you'll be unhappy, and if you don't believe it, you won't be unhappy. When you believe a lie, you will suffer, and when you don't, you won't. Let your suffering be a signal that points you back to the lie that caused it. Learn from your suffering. Learn which thoughts to not take seriously. Notice those thoughts and then return to reality, the present moment.

Could and *should* are both pretenses at control. The ego doesn't like the fact that it has so little control over life. Instead of accepting this, the ego pretends that this isn't true.

It pretends that its desires and ideas shape life or *should* be able to shape life. It believes in *could* and *should*. These two little words help create and maintain the ego's illusion of control over life, as do the ego's desires.

The ego's desires are the desires expressed in the thought-stream. These seem like *your* desires, but they are actually the desires of your programming, including the desires of your animal nature, such as the desires for comfort, safety, food, and sex. Other deeper desires stem from your true nature. You might put those desires into words at some point, but they don't initially show up in the thought-stream. They show up more subtly in your body and are felt, or known, on a deep level.

When these deeper desires are thought about or expressed, they feel right and good, unlike the ego's desires, which generally don't feel good. For instance, the thought "I want a new car" or "I want a relationship" carries a sense of lack and unhappiness, a need for something. That sense of needing something to be happy doesn't feel good. On the other hand, a deeper desire, such as the longing to expand yourself by studying or creating something, feels exciting, good, and inspiring when you put it into words and think about it. These positive feelings are how you can tell the true desires from the false ones, the true self's from the ego's.

There is nothing wrong with following the ego's desires. In fact, you are meant to, to some extent, because that's how you learn about life. It's just that the ego's desires are not what they seem to be. They are not what makes life be the way it is, although they shape life a little. The ego, however, seems to be under the impression that its desires and ideas are what shape life. This false assumption needs examining.

The ego puts itself at the center of the universe, and it sees its desires and ideas as central to that universe, when the opposite is true. The ego is not in control, and its ideas, fantasies, and desires mean little in terms of what actually shows up in life. Your ideas and desires, however, are crucial in determining how happy you will be. To the extent that you require life to match them, you will suffer. That's the truth about them.

The ego has it backwards: Your ideas and desires are not helping you be a happier and better person. Rather, they are preventing you from that. When you drop your ideas and desires, you drop into the present moment—into reality—and instantly align with your true nature and become all that you ever wanted to be: complete, happy, at peace, content, wise, and loving. You are already what you want to be! But believing that you are the *you* that desires and struggles to control life keeps you from discovering the truth about yourself.

The truth about life is that you don't need the control the ego assumes it needs, because something is in control that is good and wise and has your best interests at heart. Once you stop trying to control life, you discover that everything is already under control and always has been by a benevolent force that has you in its heart—because it is you. You are its reflection in human form and dearly beloved. Just as I, the Son, am a reflection of the Father, so are each of you.

Another false assumption is the thought "I need...." Although there are certain basic needs essential to survival, thoughts that begin with "I need" are false assumptions. The ego believes it needs things to be a certain way to be happy. These are not actual needs but imagined needs: lies. Life doesn't have to fit your ego's ideas or desires for you to be happy. That is a false assumption. Happiness is always possible, even under very difficult circumstances. The happiness I'm talking about is a deep feeling of contentment with and gratitude for life.

When you stop opposing life as it is and start embracing it, as the hero does, you fall into life—into the moment—and fall in love with life. Life is good just as it is. It is blessed. It is miraculous. It is a gift just as it is. Being alive and experiencing *whatever* you are experiencing is a great privilege.

Any experience can be gained from, no matter how hard. And most of the wisdom and many of the greatest benefits of living are won as a result of struggles and difficulties. Challenges make you strong in ways that ease cannot.

Challenges are necessary to uncover and develop the hero's latent strengths: the strength to persevere, to refrain from indulging in negative emotions and actions, to be patient, to follow a path other than the ego-driven one, to endure, to be calm and peaceful, to refrain from self-doubt and fear, to know what is true and act in accordance with that, to overcome destructive habits, and to resist destructive desires or ones that waste one's energy.

People naturally try to avoid pain and challenges, but these are necessary and intrinsic to life and therefore need to be embraced. The hero has learned to embrace challenges and not fall prey to victimization, self-pity, anger, sadness, resistance, overwhelm, hopelessness, or helplessness.

The hero also has learned that making mistakes is a natural part of life and cannot be avoided. It is how people evolve. The hero sees this and accepts this. For instance, your will is developed because of the suffering caused by giving in to your weaknesses, you learn to love because of the pain of being unloving, and you learn to be careful because of the difficulties you experienced when you weren't. Through challenges, you learn how to live, and that is what life is about: how to live from a higher place than one's ego and animal instincts.

Life is not about getting what the ego wants or thinks it needs. Life is already delivering exactly what you need: What you're getting *is* what you need. To grow in the ways you need to grow, you need whatever experience you are having.

You know what you need by noticing what is in your life now. For instance, if you are struggling in your relationship, then that is your current curriculum. The lesson might be any number of things: to accept and allow, to not accept abuse, to not judge, to trust, to compromise, to overcome anger and selfishness, to be patient, or to love, which entails all of the other lessons.

If your struggles are around supporting yourself, then that is your current curriculum. You are being asked to learn about making money as well as cultivate the inner resources to cope with a lack of it. It's also a time for discovering what you love doing and what really matters to you. It's your chance to develop your talents and uncover ones you never knew you had, because only by doing so will you find meaningful and satisfying work that will support you.

If you are struggling with health issues, then that may be a wake-up call. Is there something you need to change about how you are living your life? Your diet or other habits? Your attitude? Your lifestyle? Your relationships? Your job? Perhaps nothing has to be done except to accept and be willing to live with the limitations your health is providing. The lesson may be one of the deepest spiritual lessons of all: surrender to what is. Once you have that one mastered, you become a Master: a hero.

Life, including your life, is as it is meant to be, and wisdom is knowing this. Once you see this about life, you can relax into whatever experience you are having, make the most of it, and enjoy it for what it is and not be unhappy about what it is *not.* You have what you need because life is always providing exactly what you need for your growth and otherwise.

You may think you need to be healthy when you are not, or thin when you are not, or rich when you are not, or something else that you currently are not, but you are playing exactly the role or roles you came here to play in this drama of life and learning from them.

Many of those roles change throughout life, which is another avenue of learning: Those who are poor may become rich, and those who are rich may become poor. Those who are healthy become sick, and those who are sick may become healthy. Those who are unsuccessful may become successful, and those who are successful may become unsuccessful.

Everyone is playing the role or roles they are meant to play for the time being. Everyone is here to teach others, and everyone is here to learn:

The beautiful person teaches you to overcome your jealousy, and he or she learns about the limits of beauty.

The poor teach you compassion, and they learn inner strength.

The rich teach you about your own greed and desires, and they learn about the same.

The sick teach you to serve and remind you of your vulnerability, and they learn to receive.

The disabled teach you gratitude, and they learn about limitation.

Criminals show you how hurtful people can become when the ego is control, and they learn the depth of suffering that is possible.

Athletes teach you perseverance and endurance, and they learn the same.

The victim teaches you to not be a victim, and he or she learns the same.

Those who abuse their power teach you not to give away your power, and they learn the emptiness and pain of power executed without love.

How quickly you learn these things is up to you, but
everyone eventually learns, either in this lifetime or in
another.

Another way others are your teachers is by triggering
your negative emotions and judgments, which you need to
take responsibility for and master:

> *The beautiful woman didn't cause your jealousy — your desires
> caused it.*

> *The homeless person didn't cause your repulsion — your fear of
> being on the street did.*

> *The bad driver didn't cause your anger — your expectation that
> he or she should drive differently did.*

> *Your spouse didn't cause your hurt — your need for your
> spouse's approval did.*

For example, if you find yourself rejecting someone who is
poor, you need to look at your fear of poverty and any
judgments you have about those who are poor. Judgments
and blame are how you avoid looking at your own fear of
poverty and facing your own vulnerability. Once you do,
compassion and love can then flow. Otherwise love can't
flow to others.

You can transmute any negative emotion or judgment
into love by seeing that there is nothing to reject outside
yourself. Anything you are rejecting or judging about
someone else is about you, not the other person. *You* created
the repulsion, judgment, or negative emotion because you

rejected something within yourself, something inherent in every human being:

The greed you judge the rich for is in you too.

The overindulgence you judge the heavy person for is in you too.

The selfishness you judge your partner for is in you too.

The superficiality you judge the beauty queen for is in you too.

The laziness you judge the unemployed for is in you too.

Every human is endowed with the same flaws and the same virtues. When you can accept that what you are judging or rejecting in someone else is also within you, then you won't put others out of your heart for that. Have compassion for your own humanity, and you will be able to have compassion and love for everyone else.

It's painful to not love. Look inside and see how you prevent yourself from loving certain people, and that will free you to love, including to love yourself. When you don't love others, it's nearly impossible to love yourself because not loving makes you feel small and bad about yourself. Love, on the other hand, is proof of your greatness, your true nature, which is pure goodness.

So, you see, life doesn't need to be any different than it is. It is already being orchestrated perfectly, designed exquisitely for your growth and everyone else's. It was not designed to fit your desires and imagination, but God's. So let go and let God, as they so wisely say.

This brings us to the deepest truth, which is that there is no such thing as beautiful or ugly, successful or unsuccessful, intelligent or unintelligent, rich or poor, sick or well, or any other duality or descriptor you can think of. Although these words are necessary for communication, they don't point to anything real. They are mental constructs often utilized by the ego to support its black and white perspective, which categorizes everything and everyone as either good or bad. The ego paints in very broad brush strokes.

In truth, there is no good or bad, only what *is*. The hero loves what is, while the ego loves only what it deems to be good and rejects or avoids the rest. But everything is needed to make this world go around. Everything and everyone is equally valuable, or the world wouldn't serve the hero's growth as beautifully as it does. Life is good—all of it! It is all as it is meant to be.

Being happy requires accepting and loving all of it. To the extent that you don't, you will be unhappy. Notice how it feels in your body when you reject something. It doesn't feel good! Now notice how it feels when you accept and love something. It feels good! That is your power. If you want to feel good, you can. All you have to do is accept and love whatever *is* rather than reject it. Love reality just as it is. This is a choice.

The hero embraces life just as it is because he realizes that there is no point in doing otherwise. Opposing what *is* doesn't change a thing except one's degree of happiness. The hero has observed reality and noticed the truth: Wanting things to be different than they are right now or wanting the past to be different than it was is fruitless and only causes unhappiness. For the hero, there really is no other choice but to love what is.

Now we come to the biggest false assumption of them all: whatever comes after the words "I am." Whatever you say after those two words can only be a very small description of yourself, if it is true at all. If only the words that usually follow "I am" were just descriptions and not negative stories, as they so often are, it wouldn't be so bad: "I'm too old to learn something new." "I'm a failure at relationships." "I'm not good enough at anything." "I'm never going to be able to forgive him."

Who is this "I?" Is anything you can say about it true throughout time? That would be the test of a statement's veracity, wouldn't it? But there are few things that would pass that test. This "I" is very illusive—an illusion actually. You can't find it, and you can't tell the truth about it because it isn't real and doesn't exist. How can you accurately describe something that is an illusion except to say that it is an illusion?

The narrative about you that goes on in your head has no substance and therefore no truth. You could disregard your thoughts about "I," and you wouldn't miss a thing—except the suffering they generally produce. And remember: If a thought causes suffering, it is a lie. Suffering is how life points you away from the mind's lies.

If you look at the thought-stream, you will discover that much of your suffering comes from your "I" thoughts, from believing that this "I" is who you are. "I am (fill in the blank)" creates the false self and is largely responsible for maintaining it. If you stopped believing that this "I" is who you are, the false self would collapse, and the true self would be all that remained.

Is it so hard to believe that something else is living your life besides this "I"? It's watching the whole play of this person who believes himself or herself to be the character instead of the observer and knower of the character. What is it that can see that you are playing a character?

It's actually pretty obvious, isn't it, that you are playacting? TV, movies, and other stories give you practice observing characters playing out their roles. You know this is true of you as well. You are playing a character, and yet you know you are playing a character.

What knows this? What sees? What hears? What experiences? Is that the character or something else? If it is the character, then you wouldn't be able to be aware of the character you are playing. However, you can describe this character pretty well—and you often do. It is what is described in your thought-stream.

But the character isn't who you really are, and that's really good news because the character has flaws and an ego, which isn't very pretty sometimes. It's a good thing that who you really are is the hero, with all of the hero's qualities: strength, wisdom, contentment, compassion, insight, love, and courage.

In any moment, you can access those qualities because they are always there. The more you access them, the stronger they become, and the more those qualities become part of the character you are playing. The happy ending to the story of you is that your character becomes a hero.

You are meant to become your true self, but even then, you will still be a human being with a role to play and the traits and tendencies of the character you are playing, except that the character will be infused with love, peace, joy, wisdom, courage, and every other good quality you can imagine.

CHAPTER 4

The Strengths of the Hero

The hero's strengths are humanity's strengths, which are also the strengths of your divine nature. You are in essence divine but playing the part of a human being. Sometimes your ego gets the better of you, and the lesser qualities of your human nature show, while at other times, your best qualities shine.

Because the hero's strengths are humanity's, everyone knows them intimately. Your divine nature is not hidden or mysterious but expressed through you moment by moment, if you allow it to be. It appears as all of the qualities you admire: courage, strength, love, wisdom, discernment, joy, peace, compassion, optimism, humility, purposefulness, creativity, patience, kindness, reliability, diligence, responsibility, discipline, endurance, and adaptability.

However, what really makes the hero a hero is that she knows what quality is appropriate to the moment. She knows when to stand firm and when to surrender, when to endure and when to let go, and when to be strong and when to be gentle. Timing is everything, which is why the hero pays close attention to the moment. That is how she knows how to act and behave.

If the hero's qualities are not expressed in a way that is appropriate to the situation and balanced, they become problematic. For instance, strength is not a strength if it isn't balanced by receptivity, kindness, compassion, and a willingness to compromise when needed. The misapplication or misuse of the hero's qualities can bring destruction as much as the ego's selfishness, greed, and hatred.

The ego often distorts and corrupts the positive qualities of the hero:

Strength becomes abuse of power.

Endurance becomes rigidity or blind adherence to tradition.

Kindness becomes victimhood.

Courage becomes foolishness.

Peace becomes passivity.

Love becomes enabling.

Responsibility becomes martyrdom.

Reliability becomes stagnation.

Surrender becomes submission.

Optimism becomes blind faith.

Discipline becomes harshness.

The difference between the ego and the hero is the wisdom to apply these positive qualities in just the right measure at just the right time. You could say that life is about learning to do just that. It's as if you have been given a palette of colors, with the hero's qualities representing all the colors. Your task is to paint something beautiful rather than bring horror to the world.

The destructiveness of the misapplication of the hero's qualities is often difficult to see:

War is masked as honorable and for love of country.

Corporate greed is masked as freedom.

Materialism is masked as prosperity and the route to happiness.

Selfishness is masked as individualism.

Religious intolerance is masked as righteous action.

These things become sanctioned in society because they appear other than they actually are. If war were seen as it actually is—murder—it would be unacceptable. If corporate greed were seen as it actually is—the worship of money above all else—society would limit corporate power. If materialism were seen as it actually is—a plundering of the earth's resources—people would focus on other more meaningful values.

The hero knows when and how to act because she lives in the present, which reveals this. She is an expert at attending to what is, at being present. The ego doesn't determine the hero's actions; the flow does. When the thought-stream is no longer attended to, all that's left is the flow and responding to it. Just as the wind carries the bird, the moment carries the hero, without thought, without fear or doubt or questioning.

Whatever quality of true nature is needed in the moment simply appears. If courage is required, the hero experiences courage. If patience is required, the hero experiences that. This is how human beings are meant to live, how they are destined to live. The hero is the enlightened human.

You may think that living this way is farfetched, unrealistic, and unattainable. But you would be wrong because more and more are living this way much of the time, although you may not be aware of that.

If you met someone who is enlightened or nearly so, you would probably just think that person was very nice. You might have to know that person intimately over time before you realized there was something special about him or her. The hero is very ordinary and only stands out as being an exemplary human being. The hero is not a god with extraordinary powers or even charisma necessarily, and many spiritually advanced people are still quite flawed.

Enlightenment is not only attainable but necessary for humanity to continue and thrive. Life cannot continue as it is on this planet, or there will be no habitable planet left. This is why I am delivering this message now, not only for your personal freedom and happiness, but for the survival of humankind. The ego has been in power too long, so long that it's hard to imagine what life would be like if people actually lived in love and peace, as religious scriptures suggest.

Love your neighbor as yourself. But that isn't easy if you don't love yourself. It isn't easy to love the false self because it does things that aren't very loveable, such as complain, judge, get angry, and be selfish and unkind. When you or others are identified with the thought-stream, you and they are not so lovable. Fortunately, the false self isn't real, so it doesn't matter if you love it or not; it only matters that you see that it's false.

Everyone's false self is unlikeable to one degree or another because it's a reflection of the ego, which is the origin of every negative thought, feeling, and action. It's asking too much to love the ego. Just accept that you have one, accept that everyone has one and that you are all in the same boat. Everyone suffers from the negativity of the ego. The ego hurts you and it hurts others. The situation deserves your compassion.

Accept the ego as part of the human condition but know that you are other than that. You are the goodness that wants to be free of the negativity, the goodness that wants love and peace, the goodness that is willing to read these words and practice these teachings. That goodness is entirely lovable, and that is all you have ever truly been.

The illusion of a false self is a tricky one. It fools you into thinking that you are what your mind says you are. Oh, the mind might sometimes tell you that you are wonderful, but mostly the mind is a stream of judgment, blame, self-doubt, shame, guilt, discontentment, complaints, comparisons, or just nonsense. If that's how you feel inside, how can you love yourself and love others? It's no wonder being loving and happy is so difficult for most people.

Doesn't being happy make being loving easy? Haven't your happiest times been also your most loving ones? So *be* happy by choosing to be something other than the thought-stream. The thought-stream isn't who you are. You aren't that unhappy and unkind person. You are life itself—and it is happy to just be alive.

Can you find that place within you that is content and happy with life? If you don't listen to the mind that says otherwise, you will be able to experience that which is within you that is always and forever happy and therefore loving and at peace with life just as it is.

The hero isn't fooled by the thought-stream. The hero knows herself as something other than the character she is playing and the thoughts that character is having. The hero is aware of the character and the character's traits, talents, and foibles as well as the character's thoughts, beliefs, conditioning, fears, and desires. But the hero chooses what conditioning and drives to follow and what beliefs to believe and desires to pursue.

The hero is guided by something that is beyond the character and beyond the thought-stream, something mysterious and yet so intimate and true that it cannot be denied. Because she allows this to guide her, she is happy, life goes well, and love flows. The hero has discovered the key to happiness. And now you have too.

The key is simply this: Do not listen to the thought-stream. You are not beholden to it. You do not owe it your loyalty or attention. It is this unexamined loyalty and attention that keeps people captive to negative thoughts, limitation, fear, and every imaginable negative emotion, captive to every story you have ever told about yourself.

The price of freedom is to stop being loyal and attentive to the thought-stream. Once you realize that someone is no longer trustworthy, you stop giving that person your loyalty and attention. You stop believing that person. This is what you have to do with the stream of thoughts that masquerades as *your* thoughts. Stop trusting and believing the thought-stream. It is part of the human condition, but it does not represent who you really are.

Question each thought, and you will discover that you have never needed those thoughts in order to be you, because the real you is outside of those thoughts, observing the thought-stream and seeing the truth of what I just said. The awakening hero wakes up from identification with the thought-stream and sees the truth. Then real living can begin.

This waking up doesn't happen overnight, however. The awakening hero sees the truth and then forgets, and remembers and forgets countless times. Then one day, the truth sticks, and she remains in reality, in the here and now, and she can no longer believe the mind's stories about the past and imaginations of the future, nor its fears, desires, discontentment, self-doubts, judgments, and anger.

These mental creations belong to the human condition. They aren't part of anyone's true self. They are the face the false self wears in the world. This is why people are so predictably difficult: Everyone has the same negative false self and ego. No one is unique that way. The false self conceals the beautiful individuality and creativity of the hero, the surprising spontaneity and love that is your true nature. Believing that the false self is who you are causes all of the suffering on the planet.

The real you is replete with resources, with everything you need to be happy and fulfilled. What else do you need to get by in life other than wisdom, love, patience, perseverance, kindness, acceptance, peace, and joy? With these strengths and without the fear and other negative emotions created by thought, couldn't you handle anything? How powerful you actually are! But you don't necessarily know it. Each and every one of you has boundless untapped resources available to you. The Father does not leave you stranded. You have been given a substantial survival kit.

How ironic it is that the ego interferes with survival as much as it does, when it was designed *for* survival. The ego is indeed a survival mechanism. However, the thought-stream, which flows from the ego and conditioning, makes life's challenges more difficult than they need to be. The ego may help you survive in the midst of an attack or a cataclysm, but it does nothing for your day-to-day troubles or your happiness. The thought-stream attempts to help you navigate your life and challenges, but it fails miserably at it.

The thought-stream offers very little. For instance, let's say you just found out you lost your job. What types of thoughts are likely to go through your mind? They probably would be fears and speculations about the future: "What will I do? Will I be able to pay my bills? Will I have to move? What's going to happen to me?" These thoughts are natural, but are they useful? If they aren't useful, then they are taking your attention and energy unnecessarily, which could go somewhere more productive.

Such thoughts only add stress to a stressful situation. However, if we examine this idea more closely, is the situation actually stressful, or are the thoughts about it making it stressful? If you knew that something better than your current job would take its place, would losing your job be stressful? Probably not. What makes this situation stressful is not knowing what will happen or assuming that something you don't want is going to happen.

What if not knowing were okay with you? And what if you didn't assume a negative outcome? This situation, like so many others, may not be in your control, but you *are* in control of whether or not you are okay with not knowing the outcome and whether or not you assume a negative outcome. You have the power to choose what to conclude about any situation you find yourself in. You have always had this power, and what you decide to conclude will determine whether or not you are happy — and functional.

What if you lived one moment at a time instead of jumping into an imaginary future? What if you just stayed *here?* Is *here* so bad? And what about *now?* Is this *now* so bad? Without a negative thought about the future, there is no problem. Thoughts about the future *are* the problem.

Your mind makes up a negative future that will never be. You don't know what the future will be, but you can be sure it won't be as the mind imagines it, because the mind doesn't know what will be. It doesn't have a crystal ball. The crystal ball the mind pretends to have predicts only scary scenarios. Who needs that? The last thing you need during a time of change is to be frightened. Being scared is a highly dysfunctional state. Stress is not functional.

Change is *not* dangerous. It is normal and common. One thing you can always count on is that life will take surprising turns. Furthermore, change is often necessary for happiness. Some of the unhappiest people are those who have refused to change when life has nudged them to. Change is built into life to evolve and shape you. It is what turns the ordinary human into the hero.

When change is called for, the hero has learned to delve into her bag of resources rather than look to the thought-stream for answers or guidance. The first resource needed is a positive outlook. The hero comes to positive conclusions, if any:

All is well.

Even this is the right experience.

It must be time for a change.

This could be fun and interesting.

Let's see what happens next.

I'm sure this will work out.

Let's see what the universe has in store for me now.

This frees me to do something else.

These thoughts counteract any negative ones the mind might be churning out and prevent any stress chemicals from being released into the system, which might wear the hero down. Such thoughts shore the hero up — and they are true.

Life is an adventure that everyone is equipped to handle, especially with the help of others, who are given to you to ease your way. Everyone has the same inner resources; everyone is potentially strong, capable, and wise;

and everyone receives help from others. Life is designed to support you.

Positive thoughts such as those just mentioned make it possible to stay present in the moment, where the strengths of your true nature, including wisdom, can be accessed. Challenging times are when you most need these strengths and when, for many, they are the least accessible because of the mind's fearful messages.

If you are able to resist the thought-stream's negativity, you will gain access to the courage you need to navigate any change or difficulty. Courage is part of your God-given survival kit. It is intimately linked to optimism and cannot coexist with pessimism. This is why optimism and hope are so important. Without these, there is no courage, and without courage, facing change and trying new things is especially hard.

Human beings are creatures of habit, and when faced with necessary changes, they naturally resist. Courage makes it possible to say yes to something new, different, and unknown. However, courage is not the courage to take just *any* action, as the ego might have you do. It is the courage to be in the unknown until right action arises, and then to take that action.

The fear of change is no small hurdle. The ego is very comfortable with the familiar and uncomfortable with the unfamiliar. When faced with the unknown, the ego automatically imagines the worst. To it, danger is lurking around every corner. And that just isn't so.

Change means that different things will have to be experienced, but life is life, and different things are not actually all that different. If you've had a job before, then a different job is not that different. If you have been single before (which everyone has), then being single again is not that different. Change doesn't have to be scary. We're not talking about going to another planet, just something different on a very familiar planet.

Life is not scary, as the mind presumes, although believing the mind can make you scared. The ego overlooks all the friendly faces, new opportunities, and support that exist in your day-to-day life. Moreover, it overlooks your inborn resources, which can carry you through any experience you could possibly have. The awakening hero is meant to discover and develop these resources. But before this is possible, she must have seen that the mind's fears and version of life aren't true, since these blind one to the truth about life and block access to the hero's qualities.

Does that seem like an outrageous claim—that life isn't dangerous? Dangers *do* exist in life, but does that make life dangerous? "Life is dangerous" is a story told about life that doesn't tell the whole truth. Some moments are dangerous, but many more are not. This story leaves out all the ordinary moments as well as the moments when wonderful things show up: love, beauty, interesting new people and ideas, fun experiences, pleasures, victories, comforts, rest, creativity, inspiration, awe, joy, peace, and glimpses into your true nature.

The trouble with negative stories like "life is dangerous" is that they can take the joy out of potentially wonderful moments or cause you to miss those moments altogether. Such stories don't even help you deal with any danger you do encounter, since they keep you in a state of fear, which is a less effective state than being present.

At this point, you might be arguing that you aren't afraid of life and that you don't believe that life is dangerous, and that may be true. Nevertheless, this belief is encoded in everyone's genes. It's part of your animal nature to see life this way. Everyone who has an ego feels, on some level, that life is dangerous. Whether you have an actual thought like this or not, this fearful programming is likely to affect you unconsciously.

This programming can be counteracted with positive statements that generate hope and courage. Everyone needs such statements, especially in times of difficulty. If you have regularly practiced being positive during ordinary times, then you will be better equipped when challenging situations arise. Staying positive in the midst of difficulties will be much easier if you have practiced being positive all along.

The hero stays positive. The hero is committed to positive thoughts simply because she has seen the destructiveness of negative thoughts and the value of positive ones. Nevertheless, putting this into practice isn't so easy because the mind's negative thoughts, especially its fears, are very believable. They are meant to be. Such programming is deep and unconscious and therefore difficult to overcome without a conscientious effort.

The mind's negative thoughts aren't easily dismissed because they are infused with something that makes them very compelling: a sense of *you*. They are *your* thoughts. They have the feel of being a personal message to you from someone who knows.

Your negative thoughts also often have an urgency about them. If someone rushed up to you and excitedly whispered something in your ear, wouldn't you listen, and wouldn't you give some weight to what that person was saying? Your negative thoughts are like that. They seem true and make you feel like you have to do something about them. They contain the subliminal message: "If you don't believe this, you'll be in trouble!"

Knowing that the sense of importance and urgency in such thoughts is manufactured by programming is half the battle. However, you still have to be aware of your negative thoughts moment by moment and be diligent about not paying attention to them. It's no wonder it can take years once you have seen the truth about your thoughts to actually stop believing them and to live more in the present moment.

The hero doesn't become a hero overnight, so she has to develop patience and continued commitment to the truth to further evolve. The adventure of life cultivates the strengths of the hero slowly over time. So let's talk about patience.

One of the pitfalls on the road to becoming the hero is discouragement—losing courage and hope. Patience is the antidote to this. You can only become discouraged if you believe that something should be easier, feel differently, or not take as long as it does. Patience is born from the wisdom of seeing that everything is as it needs to be and takes as long as it takes.

Can this moment be any different than it is? Can you be any different than you are in this moment? No. The hero realizes this. This moment is what it is. Your life is what it is right now and can't be any different. It soon will be different, though, since you continue to evolve and life continues to unfold. Life is in constant motion, always moving on to the next thing, ever-evolving, sometimes in surprising ways.

That evolution and unfoldment is not primarily up to you, however, but up to something much greater than you. You play a part in your own and life's unfoldment, but a relatively small one. Your efforts are not as determinant of life as you might like to think. The idea that you create your life singlehandedly is wishful-thinking on the part of the ego. However, although your choices are not what ultimately govern life, they do determine your happiness. The choice of what you give your attention to means everything in terms of your happiness.

Patience allows you to be happy in the midst of the mind's complaints and dissatisfaction with not being able to control life. Patience comes from acknowledging a greater design and timing, which you aren't privy to but must accept. Patience is the willingness to acquiesce to Thy will. It is based on the humble recognition that you don't necessarily know what is best for yourself and others and that you aren't in control of how life shows up.

Those who are patient are wise about life. They know the truth about life, which is what makes patience and acceptance possible. Impatience, on the other hand, is an indication of being ignorant or resistant to the truth about life. It is a sign that you're caught in the ego's perspective. The antidote is seeing the truth: Life is what it is, and it can't be any way other than the way it is right now.

Wisdom is also knowing that the things that happen to you mean nothing personal about you. If your life isn't going the way you would like it to, that doesn't mean you are inadequate or that you did anything wrong. Life doesn't organize itself just to please your ego. It's not personal when life doesn't go your way.

The hero knows not to take things personally. She doesn't tell stories that revolve around herself: "I never get what I want. My life is too hard. If only I'd done that differently." The hero knows she can't know what life is up to, but she trusts that it is all good. She knows to go with the flow and have no regrets or even expectations about what lies ahead. This attitude allows her to be present.

The hero has patience not only because she knows the truth about life, but because she lives in the present moment and is therefore happy. If you are already happy, then what is there to be patient about? You aren't waiting for some future moment to make you happy. Isn't that what impatience is? You're impatient for some imagined future to arrive. But if you are happy *now*, which you will be if you are present, you won't be looking to the future to make you happy.

What makes the present moment a happy place is love. When you are present, the love and gratitude of your true nature flow toward whatever you are experiencing. If you are with others and present to them, then love flows to them. If you are alone, then love flows to whatever things and living beings are present. This flow of love is spontaneous and can only be inhibited by thoughts. Love is natural to each moment. When you experience this flow of love, you feel happy and complete.

How wonderful it is that the flow of love is in your control, or it can be. Even if you aren't experiencing it, you can call it forth by choosing to send love to people and things in your environment. You have the power to send love and therefore the power to be happy!

This is the Father's gift and the Father's message to you: Love! It is the secret to life. Earlier, I said the key to happiness is to stop giving your attention to the thought-stream. That's because when you stop being lost in thoughts about yourself, you land in the present moment, love naturally flows, and you feel happy.

You are here to learn to love, and the Father rewards you for that discovery with happiness. What a wonderful adventure this life is, to be given the task of finding a treasure that will make you eternally happy. In this sorrow-filled world, a treasure is hidden, and it lies within you. The treasure is all the beautiful qualities of your true nature — the strengths of the hero — which have been veiled by the false self. The hero's journey is this adventure of discovery, and the precious qualities, themselves, are developed by the search for this treasure.

CHAPTER 5

Navigating Challenges

"Navigating" is a perfect word to describe the way the hero moves through challenges because when you navigate a car or boat or some other vehicle, you take each moment, each twist and turn, one at a time. You are traveling on the road or on the water, one mile or stroke of the paddle at a time. You are right there, in the present moment, without a past or future, just taking it as it comes. Where you've come from has disappeared from view, and you don't know what the path ahead or your destination will be like. The only thing that is real is what you are experiencing right *now*.

Human beings are built to do a very interesting thing. They carry around a mental picture of the past and future in the midst of their present moment experience. People create stories in their minds using the imaginary past and future, and even their imaginary ideas about the present, and call this reality. They believe this imaginary, or illusory, reality *is* reality. This is the faulty map, and it gets people into trouble, into suffering.

The real map is whatever is happening now... and now... and now.... Every step of the journey is the map. Each step reveals, or points to, the next step. Like a tracker in the forest, the hero must follow the tracks and signs he comes across that point the way. Only then is the path revealed. The hero has to remain vigilant and present to the clues the present moment provides, or he will get lost.

The mind might think it knows which way to go, but it can never really know this, any more than the tracker's mind can. It isn't the mind's place to know such things. How can it? The mind is essentially a computer that processes information. How to live, how to be happy, and how to fulfill your unique destiny are not things the computer-mind can know. It can tell you how many miles are left on a trip, but it can't tell you how to be the hero of your life.

That's fine, because you have been given something else to show you the way. The Father provides you with not only the qualities of the hero, but also a means of guiding you and communicating with you. You are truly loved and cared for on this adventure. To make sure you don't lose your way, you have been given a very simple guidance system that says yes or no to various possibilities.

This yes-no guidance is like the hot and cold game you used to play as children, where a player is guided by others shouting: "You're cold... you're getting warmer... you're hot!" You can tell whether a course of action is on-course or off-course simply by noticing how you feel energetically when considering a possibility. A contracted feeling is a no, while an expanded, joyful, excited feeling is a yes.

This is as simple a guidance system as can be, but you have to use it. Just as your GPS won't get you where you want to go if you don't use it, if you don't consult or trust this inborn GPS, it can't take you where you are meant to go.

This simple yes-no guidance system is often overridden by the mind, which is always ready with a plan for what to do, when, and how. However, the mind's plan is based on conditioning and stored information, not on reality, as the internal guidance system you have been given is. Ideas and information are fine and useful at times; they just aren't enough to guide your life.

The information stored in your computer-mind is like having half a map, which is not much good, and yet it still seems like a map. If you insist on using a partial map of reality, you will only get so far. The directions from the thought-stream are like that: They take you somewhere but not necessarily where you really want to go. The thought-stream only takes you where your ego or conditioning wants you to go.

The trouble is that people assume the thought-stream is something wiser than that. If people believed there was another more trustworthy guidance system, they would use the mind only for what the mind is meant for—providing information and analysis along the way—and leave the "along the way" up to something wiser: the Heart, which is the seat of the divine self in the body.

Many have called this inborn guidance system the Heart because the expansion and contraction of this yes-no guidance system is usually felt in the chest area. This is a clue to differentiating the ego's guidance from the Heart's: The guidance occurs in very different parts of the body.

If the guidance shows up as a thought, then it is likely from the ego; if it shows up as an energetic expansion or a contraction or a download of knowing, then it is from the true guidance system. For most people, the distinction is pretty clear, but often their mind or other people's minds talk them out of believing their true guidance system. Minds have a way of sounding very convincing.

When things go badly as a of result of following the ego's guidance, people often blame God, when the Father had a better plan in mind for them all along. This is not to say that there aren't challenges even when you follow the true guidance system, but those challenges will be specifically designed for your growth, not just to get you back on track. When you are off-course, life erects roadblocks to get you to change course.

These roadblocks can be quite painful—and they're meant to be—because they are telling you: "What you *think* you want or what you think you *should* do is not what you need. Follow your Heart." Suffering is meant to point you in a different direction and get you to ask, "What do I really want?" It is meant to get you to follow your joy, not your thoughts.

The only things that make following your joy difficult are your ideas and fears and other people's. And yet, what are ideas and fears? They are a faulty map of reality—a map of an imaginary reality. People are often so sure they know what the right thing to do is and how that will turn out, but they don't. No one does. Everyone is driving blind in this life. No one knows anything, until they do. To pretend that you know is to put your faith in a faulty map.

The hero is willing to drive blind with no other map but reality: the present moment. The guidance system the hero follows is joy, which is felt as a yes to moving a certain way in the moment. What am I feeling moved to do now? And now? And now? This sounds highly impractical to the mind, but it isn't at all. Following the mind's instructions moment to moment, as most people do, is no more practical: "Do this now, then do that, then you should do that," commands the voice in your head. How does that voice come up with those instructions? It deduces them up from the programming.

The hero does what is in front of him to do, naturally and fluidly. When a challenge arises, the hero still does whatever is in front of him to do. Challenging times are not lived any differently than easy ones. Both call for the same equanimity and straight-forward, rational action needed in the moment.

When you live this way, challenges are not necessarily so challenging. What makes a situation more challenging than it needs to be are the fears and ideas about what that difficulty is assumed to mean: "I'll never find love again." "I'll be homeless." "I'll die." "I won't be able to cope." "I won't be happy." The hero doesn't fall prey to such stories about what might happen. These are imaginations and only waste and scatter one's energy, just when energy and focus are most needed.

The hero has the discipline and inner strength to refrain from such negative stories. He knows there is never a time when negative thoughts are useful. In difficult times, steering clear of negative thoughts is essential. During such times, many discover the importance of staying positive, and they learn to practice being positive because they recognize that doing otherwise would be to sink the ship. Staying afloat in hard times requires the buoy of hope.

Hope gives courage and makes it possible to cope. When you lose hope, you lose courage and the ability to cope: You become dis-couraged. Discouragement lasts only as long as you believe a negative thought, while courage, because it is a quality of your true nature, is everlasting. As soon as a discouraging thought is dropped, your innate courage shines through. What a gift courage is! It isn't something you have to develop, but what naturally arises when you stop believing your thoughts.

Hope is another gift from the Father. It is built into the human to have hope, even under the direst of circumstances. "Hope springs eternal" expresses this truth. Within you is a wellspring of hope—and love and peace and joy. Hope rises up in difficult times to support you and counteract the discouragement, despair, and hopelessness of the ego when it feels most powerless.

When the ego doesn't get what it wants or when you lose something or someone dear to you, the ego falls into despair and other negative emotions. It feels powerless and defeated. But these feelings, however real they may seem, are never the truth. They are the false map. They are telling you lies: "You will never be happy again. This is too much to handle. Your life is over. Nothing will ever be right again."

The beauty of this life you have been given is that none of your negative feelings tell the truth, while the positive ones—hope, peace, joy, and love—do. You are meant to discover this truth about life. Negative feelings are a mirage created by the mind.

Hope is the truth because things are always changing and moving on to something new. With every death or loss come many new beginnings, new births. Life is unstoppably producing more life. It can't help itself. And the qualities of the hero, including happiness, love, and peace, are always available, no matter what the circumstances. You are always strong enough to cope with whatever happens in life. You only need to realize this.

Not only do things naturally move on to something new, but you are likely to have become a better human being for having gone through the fire of your trials. You are bound to have become stronger, more positive, and better able to cope with any future difficulties. Challenges transform you into the hero that each of you is meant to be.

You are meant to come away from a challenge with greater wisdom, patience, compassion, endurance, inner strength, and a greater capacity to refrain from negative emotions and stories. If you don't learn these things, you will continue to suffer even after the difficult situation is over. The remaining bitterness, resentment, sadness, and other unpleasant emotions become your next challenge until you overcome them. If you don't master these feelings, they will be the master of you, and you'll have little peace and happiness. If you don't turn your lemons into lemonade, you'll be stuck with lemons, stuck in a challenge of your own making.

When you are going through a crisis, negativity is an indulgence you cannot afford; there is no room for negative stories, self-pity, hopelessness, fear, guilt, regret, resentment, revenge, or anger. You have to find another way to cope than indulging in these because they will take you down. People who have successfully faced extreme situations got by, by not indulging in mental and emotional negativity. They also learned to take one moment at a time and focus their attention on whatever was in front of them, not farther down the road.

What you focus your attention on is critical because your attention is like a spotlight: Whatever you turn it toward becomes your experience, your reality. If you turn it toward something unreal, such as the ego's fears, negative feelings, or its *coulds* and *shoulds*, the ego's world will become your reality. Your fears, other feelings, and mistaken beliefs will seem real. But if you give your attention to what is actually real, here and now, and not to any unnecessary thoughts, you will gain access to every resource you need to cope with *this moment*—which is all you ever need.

Trying to cope with imagined future moments or change moments that have already passed is fruitless and a waste of energy. More importantly, if your focus is on the past or the future, you won't have access to the hero's qualities, which are only available in the here and now. For this reason, staying present is the key to getting through any challenge, and also to being happy.

You can get through anything if you take one moment at a time. For example, if you have to have surgery, you get up that morning and get ready. How difficult is it to take a shower and put your clothes on? How difficult is it to drive to the hospital? How difficult is it to wait in the waiting room? How difficult is it to get wheeled into the operating room? How difficult is it to be anesthetized? How difficult is it to wake up in the hospital bed afterwards? You get the picture. The only way any of these moments can be difficult is if your fears and worries make them so.

One moment at a time is all reality ever is: one slice of time, gone in an instant and replaced by another slice of time. All you ever have to do is get through that one slice of time. Most slices are ordinary and what to do is obvious. Only a relatively few moments are intense or crisis-ridden, and even those pass quickly into something else. Even with those, what to do is often obvious.

The mind makes life complicated and unpleasant by fearing, doubting, and obsessing about every possibility and option, while most moments can be handled easily enough without much thought. People think they have to figure out what to do in imagined future moments. But the hero lets the future take care of itself, because he knows the future never actually arrives. In reality, all there ever is, is one moment moving naturally and gracefully into the next, with or without the mind's ceaseless thoughts.

The mind thinks it has to manage every moment or life will go nowhere or fall apart, while quite the opposite is true: The more the mind is involved in trying to manage life, the more complicated and trying life becomes. The intellect is not the problem but, rather, the aspect of the mind that has been co-opted by the ego: the voice in your head. It is the voice of self-doubt, hysteria, fear, anger, judgment, and blame. How can it possibly manage your life well?

The stories people tell about what they are going through make life more difficult than it needs to be. When people tell a story defining their experience as terrible, that story becomes their experience. Words are powerful because they determine your inner experience, and your inner experience *becomes* your experience. Focusing on a story creates feelings, which are an inner experience, and that inner experience overshadows reality—the actual present moment experience. You become lost in an unreal inner world and out of touch with what is real, right in front of you.

People live in an internal world of their own making, created by their stories. This internal world is the world of the ego, and it is maintained by the thought-stream. If you stop believing this thought-stream, you land in reality and have a very different experience of life.

In reality, there is just this moment and nothing else. This is the enlightened human's experience. It is the experience of the eternal now, of life at its truest and most real. In any moment, there might be something to do or say, but there is no problem because there is no story. No good/bad duality exists either, because that duality and every other one are the mind's machinations. Without such dualities, desires drop away, and with them, fear.

In the moment, there is only what *is*, and the hero considers that to be good. It is all good—all God. And what would be the point of seeing it any other way? Why would you choose to suffer when you see that you don't have to?

Once you learn the secret to happiness, you don't go back to being unhappy, except when you've been temporarily taken in by the thought-stream. It is your destiny to live in the moment and leave the false reality behind. It is your destiny to be happy.

One of the most powerful tools the awakening hero has is gratitude. It is the way out of discouragement, despair, and every other difficult emotion. The hero learns to feel gratitude throughout the day for the wonderful little things in life that are such a gift and so often taken for granted by the ego.

The sun is shining! Deep gratitude. Another day on this amazing planet! Deep gratitude. The birdsong! Deep gratitude. Another day with the beloved dog! Deep gratitude. A good night's sleep! Deep gratitude. The ability to walk and talk and do things! Deep gratitude. Meeting with a good friend! Deep gratitude. A fly's ability to cling to the ceiling! The bird's ability to fly! The sky's ability to rain! Awe and wonder! These and countless other things are reasons for ongoing gratitude. This *is* life—these simple things. Life is full of wonders, and they are there just for you, for your pleasure. This and every moment is replete with them—and complete.

Gratitude opens the Heart and makes all other qualities of your true nature accessible. The feeling of gratitude is a feeling of happiness, love, and peace. The fact that you can create these positive feelings by simply noticing or naming what you are grateful for makes the practice of gratitude a very handy and powerful tool for your transformation.

It takes little time to notice or name what you are grateful for. When practiced daily, this can become a way of being in the world. Instead of giving your attention to the thought-stream, try noticing and naming what you are grateful for throughout your day, and this will change your life. A potent formula for happiness is to replace thinking about yourself with gratitude.

No matter what kind of challenge you are experiencing, gratitude and a recognition of the greater reality surrounding that difficulty will help you cope with it. There is much more to any moment than whatever may be unpleasant about it, and always much to be grateful for. Even when it seems like your life is falling apart, the sun still shines, the birds still sing, you still have the capacity to love, people are still kind, and beauty is still everywhere. The same wondrous world exists and is there to support you.

If you are experiencing physical pain, notice what is here besides the pain and your thoughts and feelings about it. What else is here that you can be grateful for? If you are experiencing sadness, anger, hurt, or any other unpleasant emotion, notice what else is here that you can be grateful for. If you are caught in memories of the past or fears of the future, notice what you can be grateful for right now. What else is here besides the story of your difficulty? What are you seeing, hearing, sensing, and intuiting? Notice the subtle experience of your divine self rejoicing in life just as it is.

You can always be grateful that whatever you are experiencing isn't more challenging than it is—that the headache isn't worse, that you broke only one leg, that you are as young as you'll ever be, that you have what you do have. Gratitude is a practice of seeing the glass as half full instead of half empty. It's a matter of acknowledging what *is* here instead of focusing on what is not. What *is* here is real; what is not here is not real. What resources are here? What support is here? What love is here? What beauty is here? What peace is here?

You can even be grateful for the challenge because that has its gifts. The greatest gifts are born from the greatest challenges, and no other way, really. In this world, growth is accomplished through trials, and this has to be accepted or you will suffer more than you need to. No one escapes challenges. The hero knows this and doesn't take them personally. They happen to everyone, and even they are good.

The hero asks, "How might this challenge be serving my growth?" He might not have an answer right away, but the question reframes the experience, turning the so-called curse into a blessing. If God is good and goodness is behind life, then even difficult situations must have their usefulness. And so they do.

If you've lived long enough, you have realized the transformative power of challenges:

Being sick makes you appreciate being well.

Losing someone reveals the strength of your love for that person and of love in general and the eternalness of that love.

Having little shows you that happiness doesn't depend on having but on being.

Losing your possessions reveals what you possess that can't be taken away.

Getting old humbles you, softens your heart, and teaches you what true beauty is.

Making mistakes makes you wise.

Death shows you that you are not your body.

Furthermore, all of these challenges increase your compassion. Life is so good that it even gives you gifts while it gives you hardships.

Your greatest resource is something you might not even be aware of. It is what is aware of everything you are aware of. What is aware of a thought? What is aware of a feeling? This is a great mystery, isn't it? That which is aware, that which is looking out of your eyes and living your life is who you really are. You know it well. It's been with you all your life, and without it, all experience would be impossible. *You* would be impossible. It is so close to you that it is easily overlooked. Like a fish that doesn't know it lives in water, you don't notice the real you. It remains the silent watcher and experiencer of all you do.

In the here and now, you discover what a hero you actually are. That aware, spacious being that is looking out of your eyes is always in perfect equanimity and perfect peace. Flowing from that space is love, compassion, gratitude, and acceptance. This mysterious space that you are has qualities, and they are those of the hero.

The hero is not so substantial after all. It is not a he or a she, young or old, fat or thin, single or married. To be seen, the hero must wear a costume, but the hero is not the costume, any more than an actor is what he or she pretends to be. The real you is what animates the character you are playing. And it is formless.

What is even more miraculous is that this hero is the same inside every human being! You are this hero, and so is everyone else. The same essence is behind every costume, living every life. This great mystical truth is not actually hidden very well, and at the end of the hero's sojourns on earth, it is not hidden at all. This is why the hero is able to be so happy and carefree, even under duress, because the truth about life is very good indeed. It couldn't be better. Life is a celebration of life, or it can be.

CHAPTER 6

Mastering Negative Emotions

The hero seeks mastery over her emotions because she knows that unmanaged emotions destroy one's chances for happiness. Negative emotions and joy are incompatible. You can have your negative emotions or you can have joy, but not both.

Most of the time, for most people, this doesn't seem like a choice: You just feel something and react. You can't help yourself. But the hero knows the results of reacting without considering the consequences and learns self-restraint. The hero doesn't let negative feelings take over and mar her inner climate or relationships.

Expressing emotions in harmful ways or even harboring them is a mistake, but an understandably human one. Human beings were created to have feelings, and unfortunately those feelings didn't come with instructions or an on-off switch. So people have no choice but to learn about their feelings through trial and error. Feelings are one of the greatest challenges of human existence and also a central part of the human experience.

The difference between the hero and many others is that the hero learns from her mistakes. She doesn't keep doing the same things that don't work just because she feels like it or knows no other way. The hero takes responsibility for her internal state and actions and adjusts her behavior accordingly. This may sound obvious, but you can find countless examples of people hurting themselves and others repeatedly and not changing their behavior. That's like throwing yourself against a wall again and again without realizing you can just stop doing that.

The problem may be, in part, that people don't realize they can stop, or they believe they can't. They feel out of control and at the mercy of their feelings. They understand so little about emotions that they don't even realize their emotions can be managed. Believing that emotions can be mastered is the first step of self-mastery.

Another reason people continue to hurt themselves and others emotionally is that they don't *want* to stop. This sounds ludicrous, but it is unfortunately true. The ego in them doesn't want to stop, even while the goodness in them does.

When the ego has the upper hand, it does some terrible things. The ego takes pleasure in doing hurtful things if it believes those things will give it the upper hand, exact revenge, or obtain power or something else it wants. The ego feels justified in having negative feelings; after all, it created that justification with its stories. As a result, it sees its feelings and actions as worth any trouble they create. Because the ego feels entitled to its feelings, it takes a kind of righteous pleasure in being awful. It also doesn't see any other option.

What the ego overlooks is the price that is paid, not only in bad karma and ill will from others, but also internally — to one's self-esteem. With every negative emotion the ego nurses inside or expresses hurtfully, it digs itself deeper and deeper into a hole of hate, self-loathing, and worthlessness. When people behave badly, is it any wonder they don't feel good about themselves?

This is a no-brainer, as they say, and a bit of a pun, as those caught in this are acting without a brain, without the rational side of their brain anyway. To the rational mind, this vicious cycle is clear: hate leads to self-hate, which leads to more hate and more self-hate. But to the irrational ego, bad behavior is just normal, an accepted and unquestioned way of being. People in their egos can't imagine being any other way, and many don't want to be. A world in which people's egos are in control is a pretty nasty place.

The change you want to see in the world must start at home. It's an inside job, which the hero willingly takes on because she recognizes the importance of this. So she makes a commitment to emotional mastery. Once you have realized mastery is possible, the second step in accomplishing this mighty task is commitment.

Commitment requires dedicating yourself to being vigilant about your emotional state moment to moment, or not much is likely to change. The ego is a formidable opponent and doesn't release its hold without a lot of diligence on your part. This willingness to look inside yourself, take responsibility for your feelings, and summon your will to make different choices than you have before comes with spiritual maturity.

Many "hang out" for a very long time knowing they need more self-mastery and wanting that but not being willing to dedicate themselves to it moment to moment. As you all know, there is often quite a gulf between wanting to improve yourself and actually doing something about it. So people often stay stuck in negative emotions, feeling victimized by their own feelings and possibly blaming God for their suffering, without accepting that self-mastery is what life is all about and realizing that they have been given every resource they need to accomplish this.

Self-mastery begins with learning to observe your thoughts. Without a practice of meditation, this is a nearly impossible task, or impossibly slow. I cannot stress this enough. Meditating an hour or more daily will make learning to observe your thoughts much easier and more efficient than trying to do this as you go about your day, which is part of self-mastery as well.

So a practice of both meditation and mindfulness throughout your day is the way to begin to experience some freedom from the suffering caused by thoughts and feelings. Much has already been written about meditation by this author and others, so I will refer you to other writings, particularly *From Stress to Stillness* by this author.

The purpose of meditation is to minimize the frequency and strength of your thoughts. Then getting some distance from them becomes much more possible. What I mean by distance is quite literal. When you aren't observing your thoughts, you are likely to be identified, or merged, with them. A regular practice of meditation produces some distance between you and a thought so that the thought can be seen as something separate from you. This *you* that is able to observe a thought happens to be the real you. When you are merged with a thought, on the other hand, you *are* the thought and there's no *real* you in the picture, only the conditioned *you*.

Thoughts are conditioning, so when you believe your thoughts, you become the conditioned self and lose touch with your real self. As a result of the distance from thoughts developed by meditation, the real self comes back into the picture. The real you is what is aware of thoughts and of everything else. The ego can't be aware of thoughts because the ego is, in essence, itself a thought. The ego belongs to the conditioned self and has no awareness of its own.

The conditioned self, including the ego, isn't actually a self at all, which is why it is also referred to as the false self. The true self is the only real self and the only thing living your life, but the true self allows identification with the false self to occur, since that is part of being human.

Because the real you is supremely wise and rational, it can see what is true or untrue about a particular thought, which isn't possible when you are identified with that thought. When you are identified, you are believing the thought unquestioningly. That results in moving through life unconsciously, with your conditioning running you. Once you achieve some distance from your thoughts, however, you gain access to the rationality and wisdom of your true self.

This is the wisdom that guides the hero. She realizes that without some distance from her thoughts she can't be the hero. She becomes the hero by achieving this distance. Meditation makes commitment to emotional self-mastery possible because it creates the necessary distance from thoughts that allows the awakening hero to not become defeated before she even begins.

Without a practice of meditation, waking up out of identification with the mind and its "virtual reality" is very difficult. Even if you've encountered teachings similar to this one about the untrustworthiness and uselessness of the thought-stream, without having developed some distance from your thoughts through meditation, you would no doubt have difficulty applying that understanding.

Others can't do this for you, nor can reading books. They can only point to the truth. In the end, you have to summon your will to make some important choices. The first choice is to practice meditation daily. The second is to be mindful throughout your day, which requires being conscious of your internal and sensory experience moment to moment.

Being mindful, or present, is challenging because it runs contrary to how you have been programmed as human beings, since your default state is to be lost in thought. To counteract this pull of thoughts, will is required.

The goal of mindfulness is to bring awareness to the habit of identifying with thought and to choose otherwise. When you are lost in thought, notice that and choose to put your attention on the here and now, on what you are sensing in your environment and body, both with your five senses and on a more subtle energetic level, which includes intuitions, inspiration, and other nudges from the Heart.

This may sound easy enough, but the magnetism of the thought-stream is great, and identifying with those thoughts is often automatic. Furthermore, some thoughts are particularly "sticky" and difficult to disregard. Those thoughts are your cutting edge, spiritually speaking. They are the thoughts that keep you tied to the illusion that you are what you are not. They are the ones that produce negative feelings and a sense of being small, powerless, and inadequate, such as: "No one ever likes me." "I can't do anything right." "I'm not smart enough." "Life is too hard." "I'm not pretty enough." "I'm always screwing up."

None of these things are true, of course. They are true relative only to some imaginary ideal. They are stories the mind made up. Everyone has such thoughts, and they do no one any good. They create the false self and aren't even necessary for you to be the character you are playing. Without these thoughts, the character will still be the character, but a much happier and more productive one. So you lose nothing when you lose your negative thoughts.

If only you could just lose them! That's where investigation, or inquiry, comes in. To become free of negative thoughts that are charged with emotion requires patient examination. The catch, as you can imagine, is that when you are identified with your thoughts, you aren't in a position to examine them because there's no distance between you and them and no will to investigate them. You are stuck with your negativity and suffering until you see that you aren't.

This is where suffering is your friend. The only reason people suffer emotionally is because they are identified with these useless and untrue thoughts. Once you know that and once you notice you are suffering, you can use that suffering to wake yourself up out of identification with your thoughts by choosing to ask the question: "What have I been telling myself that is causing these negative feelings?"

If you don't have the opportunity to do this on the spot, then take time before you go to bed, possibly every night for a while, and write down every thought you can come up with that is behind your feelings. This half of the exercise, alone, is quite powerful.

Now look each thought squarely in the face (this is your true self doing this) and question the veracity of each one. You will discover, one by one, how ridiculously sweeping the mind's statements are: No one screws up all the time. No one is without people who like them. No one is not smart enough. Smart enough for what? Everyone is smart enough to be who they are.

If you do this regularly enough, you'll see the same thoughts coming up again and again, like clockwork, right on schedule. The egoic mind is like a computer, and it spits out the same thoughts repeatedly, predictably. If you have believed a thought in the past, then that thought will be part of the mind's repertoire. When you stop believing that thought, it drops off the list.

Making note of the beliefs that still catch you up will weaken their power to get you to identify with them, and they will eventually subside. You may have to do this exercise often and for quite some time to diminish the strength of these thoughts, but it will be worth your while and become much easier over time.

The value of this inquiry and examination is not only that you will no longer be plagued by such thoughts, but you won't have to live with the feelings they generate. Once your inner climate and the emotional atmosphere around you become more positive, your experience of life will begin to transform.

In realizing that you, and only you, create your emotions, you are empowered, because that means that you, and only you, can make yourself happy. Happiness is in your control! People are under the impression that others make them feel a certain way—happy, loved, sad, angry—when the truth is that other people can only affect you if you allow them to.

Let's take a moment to examine how cleverly you create your inner experience with your thoughts. For instance, if someone says to you, "You really should lose some weight," there are an infinite number of ways you could react inside and respond on the outside. Often people respond politely on the outside, because they're taught to do that, but suffer or seethe on the inside, without realizing that they, themselves, are creating the suffering or seething, not the other person.

In this example, you might create a feeling of sadness by telling yourself: "He's right. I look terrible." Or you might create a feeling of anger by telling yourself: "What a jerk. Who is he to talk?" Or you might create a feeling of victimization by telling yourself: "Everyone is always criticizing me." Or you might create a sense of self-righteousness or superiority: "He is so unenlightened." The possible conclusions, as I said, are endless, and most people come to a string of them, resulting in a variety of feelings. More positively, you could create a feeling of inner peace by telling yourself: "He must be having a bad day" or "He's believing his judgments right now, which isn't a very happy place, so I'll send him some love."

You will never be able to do anything about what other people say or do or how they feel about you, since you have no control over that and therefore no responsibility for that. However, you do have control over your own inner climate by becoming aware of what you are saying to yourself in response to what others say or do or feel. For that, you are responsible.

This is wonderful news. It means you can be happy under any circumstance, because the same is true for the events in your life: They don't have to determine your inner climate. You determine your inner climate either by unconsciously falling into your usual negative conclusions or by consciously choosing your own conclusions.

Once you've gotten a good look at the usual conclusions your mind comes up with by writing down some of the negative things you say to yourself, then it's time to rewrite some of these conclusions. So next, make a list of some positive things you might have said to yourself instead, or things you might say to yourself next time in a similar situation. Then when the usual negative thoughts arise, you will be prepared with positive statements that can neutralize the negative thoughts before they turn into feelings.

Here are some examples of statements you could draw from in the future when faced with people or situations that would usually trigger negative feelings:

He's probably having a bad day.

I can understand how she might feel that way.

I can let that go.

I understand and forgive him for that.

It doesn't matter.

I don't need to be perfect.

There's nothing I can do about that.

I'm doing the best I can.

He's doing the best he can.

I choose to send love instead.

No problem.

All is well.

It's not important.

It will work out.

This, too, shall pass.

Everything is unfolding as it needs to.

It's none of my business.

I'll leave that up to God.

Delete that thought.

Peace, peace, peace!

What you're seeking are sentences or phrases that help you relax and be at peace in the midst of a mind that is trying to stir up your emotions. The advantage of being aware of your negative thoughts and neutralizing them in this way is that you can arrest the negative train of thoughts before it becomes a train wreck of feelings. The sooner you can disengage from your negative thoughts the better. If you allow them to continue, you will have feelings to deal with, not just thoughts.

As for dealing with emotions, it is neither helpful to repress nor express negative feelings. You may need to discuss an issue with someone that caused you to feel a certain way, but that is very different from expressing or venting the feeling itself. Acting out or reacting emotionally, and even announcing how you feel is never helpful. The distinction between expressing or venting feelings and rationally talking about an issue that triggers your feelings without making those feelings central is illustrated in the following example:

Emotionally charged and unproductive: *It makes me so angry when you leave your clothes all over the floor! I can't stand it! You're so inconsiderate!*

Rational and productive: *I would appreciate it so much if you wouldn't leave your clothes on the floor.*

The subject of expressing emotions is widely misunderstood. Many people assume that verbalizing every passing feeling and letting their feelings out is a healthy way to process their feelings. However, sharing how you feel at every turn with others often results in creating more emotions within you and within others, since few people are able to share how they feel skillfully. A better strategy is to take responsibility for creating your feelings, deal with them within yourself as much as possible, and only engage with others about your feelings when there is a purpose for doing so, and then only unemotionally.

So when is sharing how you feel purposeful? It might be purposeful in negotiating about household tasks or other differences between you and your partner. And, obviously, if something is going on emotionally between you and your partner, you need to discuss that in order to resolve it. But what needs to be discussed is how to resolve it, not "how I feel and how you make me feel." A more productive discussion would be about how you could work this out together for the good of the relationship, so everyone is happy: "What resolution can we come to that we both can live with?"

If your partner is triggering your feelings, notice that, take responsibility for those feelings, and try to dissolve them by investigating the mistaken beliefs and conditioning behind them. If necessary, present the problem to your partner to be solved jointly: "This is a problem for me, and I'm doing what I can to change how I feel and react to this. Is there something you're willing to do to make this easier for me?" Or you might simply ask: "What can we do about these differences?"

If someone is behaving abusively toward you, then sharing how you feel is imperative. You need to tell that person, in a non-emotional moment, that this behavior isn't acceptable and that if he or she continues to behave that way, you'll have to leave the relationship. It is important to address this issue at a time when you can both discuss this rationally or when a mediator is present.

Another time when sharing how you feel is imperative is if someone is regularly criticizing and judging you. You need to do your best to not take those criticisms personally *and* you need to notify that person of the effect those judgments are having on you, that they interfere with your ability to feel loving and are therefore damaging to the relationship. To make this point, you don't need to express anger at the other person, because that will only inflame him or her. If feelings can't be discussed rationally, then you might need a mediator, such as a therapist, to help you sort out the problems between you.

Expressing anger and even sadness within relationships is often a way that one person tries to manipulate another. Expressing or venting feelings is like dropping a grenade in the middle of a relationship: The atmosphere can explode into any number of other emotions. The emotional intensity can become so uncomfortable that someone gives in to the other's demands just to make peace. This is no way to negotiate. Learning to negotiate with your partner is an important skill. For further understanding about how to do this and about relationships in general, I refer you to this author's book *Choosing Love*.

The alternative to repressing or expressing a negative emotion is allowing it to be there and being curious about it and willing to find out more about it. If allowed to just be, most negative emotions dissipate rather quickly. What gives them strength and a longer life is thinking about them.

When a negative emotion is triggered, your ego, through the thought-stream, immediately tries to further justify that emotion by building a case for feeling the way you do. The thought-stream becomes filled with stories about the past and sweeping generalizations that represent only part of the truth: "There he goes again. He makes me so angry. He always does that. He never respects my needs. He's so inconsiderate. He doesn't appreciate all I do for him!"

When a negative emotion is triggered, the most important thing to do is to defuse it by not going into further thought about it. If you let your mind take over, the emotions will build, and you'll soon feel like you have a very big problem on your hands. The only real problem is that you've created a firestorm of emotion inside yourself.

Negative emotions are empowered by thinking about them and disempowered by not thinking about them. Not giving your attention to the thought-stream while you are feeling something is not repression but simply good emotional hygiene, something every child should be taught.

Feelings are natural and normal, but they aren't meant to rule you and determine your actions. Negative emotions come from the more primitive side of your brain. They are dysfunctional and don't serve humanity in any way. They need to be defused, not pumped up.

The way to defuse negative emotions is quite simple, but it requires making a conscious choice to not give the thought-stream your attention. The default for humans is to remain unconscious and let the thought-stream lead them down the path of least resistance, which is a place you really don't want to go. You are going against your programming when you choose to just be with a negative emotion rather than feed it with more thoughts.

Paradoxically, being with the experience of a negative emotion in your body disempowers it. This is so because you can't put your attention in two places at once: You are either thinking about the emotion and feeding it with more thoughts or giving your attention to the emotion itself—to the experience of it in your body. The experience of the emotion is reality, what is *actually* happening. The thought-stream, on the other hand, represents and maintains the ego's illusory reality, the one in which you exist as the false self.

Negative emotions are what make you feel so bad about yourself. They make you feel small and keep you identified with the false self instead of realizing the beautiful being that you are. Every time you indulge in negative emotions and the thoughts that create them, you strengthen the false self; when you do the opposite, you return Home.

Returning to your true self is just a matter of being with what is real, which is the bodily experience of the feeling in the moment. When you turn your attention to the experience of an emotion in the body, you are connecting with reality, and so your mind is likely to quiet some.

The emotion itself is neither good nor bad; it's what people do with it that makes it good or bad. Emotions are just part of being human and don't need to be eliminated. They just need to be managed in a way that doesn't cause pain to yourself or others. You master your negative emotions so that they don't become the master of you.

Mastering negative emotions is a matter of befriending them. By befriending, I simply mean that you neither go to war with them nor indulge them. Instead, you make space for them to be and listen to what they have to say: What are the mistaken beliefs behind those emotions? And what are the beliefs and emotions underlying those beliefs? If it's anger, what thoughts "made" you angry? And what other beliefs and emotions underlie those thoughts?

In other words, instead of automatically identifying with the thought-stream, examine and question the thoughts in the thought-stream. Once you see how untrue those thoughts are, the feelings will eventually dissipate. Sometimes just being with a negative emotion, without any examination at all, is all that is needed to defuse it.

Being with a negative emotion simply means allowing it to be there and becoming aware of the experience of the emotion in your body, without repressing that emotion or acting it out. When you do that, you often discover that the complex of feelings and beliefs behind that emotion developed from some childhood event or experience. That discovery can be a very important one and very healing.

Awareness heals. Awareness of the negative feelings, of the thoughts behind the feelings, and the origin of those thoughts and feelings heals. The awareness that you bring to thoughts and feelings *is* who you are. You are what is experiencing everything and what is aware of everything. In fact, you are everything! Everything that you experience is happening within this mysterious Awareness that you are, and everything is made of that same stuff: consciousness.

The hero aligns herself with Awareness by being very present in the body and senses and therefore present to reality. From there, emotions, including negative ones, are an interesting and rich aspect of being human — one more thing to experience that is coming and going in consciousness.

The hero learns to respond to negative emotions with acceptance, compassion, curiosity, and dispassion. Negative emotions are part of the marvelous play of life but not given any meaning beyond being a sensory experience. The hero knows that negative emotions, like all sensory experiences, quickly fade into nothingness if they are allowed to just be as they are in the body, without expressing them.

CHAPTER 7

The Hero's Beliefs

The hero does have beliefs, but they are aligned with reality. They aren't made up by the mind or handed down from others but known to be true, either because those beliefs are obviously and simply true, like "the sky is blue," or because those beliefs have proven to be true through contact with another dimension of himself.

The hero—and everyone, really—lives in several dimensions at once. The hero is aware of this, while others tend not to be. These other dimensions inform and nourish him. As a result, he knows things that others do not or don't realize they know. What the hero knows is no less real or true than the type of knowing that can be verified by the senses, but it is different.

If the only beliefs the hero relied on were ones that were provable by the five senses, he could not be the hero, since what is most basic and true about life can't be known through the five senses. Those who don't venture beyond the five senses are left, seemingly, with little to guide them. And yet, they are still guided internally, as is everyone. No one lives outside what is true about life, whether they believe the truth or not, or even if they believe the opposite. The truth is what is true and immutable about reality, and no one's beliefs or non-belief can change that.

The five senses only go so far in informing people of reality. If all human beings had to navigate life were their five senses, they wouldn't be that different from the animal kingdom. But you have something animals and other life forms do not: self-awareness. This enables you to sense the truth about life and about who you are. This truth is generally hidden, but not so well hidden that it can't be uncovered, which at a certain point, it is meant to be.

The way the truth is uncovered is by using another sense, which some have called the sixth sense. For simplicity and lack of a better term, I will call it that also. Just as there are sounds beyond the range humans can hear, there are worlds, or dimensions, beyond the one humans can sense. These dimensions exist whether or not you are aware of them. I am speaking to you from one such dimension.

The point is, you will never discover the truth about life or about who you are with your five senses. In fact, these senses contribute to the illusion that who you are is a separate, limited self. But that is as it's meant to be. Until a certain point in your evolution, you aren't supposed to be privy to the truth. Only when it is time are you made aware of your inherent divinity.

At a certain point, the sixth sense becomes more active. When that happens, you begin to receive information about reality that you never had access to before. You discover that the knowledge received from the sixth sense, as with the five senses, is relatively consistent from one person to another. This is comforting: There's some solidity to the subtle realms after all. It's just not the solidity the mind would like.

Those who haven't experienced knowing on more subtle levels naturally question what others have discovered more subtly. And why would or should anyone believe something that is outside their experience? You probably wouldn't either. So if you are experiencing these more subtle realms, don't worry about whether others experience things the way you do. You are only responsible for your own experience, and you must be true to that.

Just know that when some ability to sense the subtle world opens up, it is time for you to discover the truth. It means that your lifetimes of returning to earth or some other physical dimension are numbered. You are nearing the end of your physical lifetimes. You will continue on, however, in other dimensions that are very rich and rewarding indeed.

When the sixth sense opens up, you may develop an ability to see into these dimensions, communicate with beings in them, or sense these dimensions in other ways. Many are able to travel in other dimensions and gain information that way. But to discover the truth about life, you don't have to travel to another dimension because your being, itself, is interdimensional. Other dimensions, in a sense, exist inside you and can be accessed from within.

Your body-mind is a sensing device, an antennae, both for this dimension, through the five senses, and other dimensions, through the sixth sense. Whether you realize it or not, these senses are continually informing you about physical reality and other dimensional realities. And whether you realize it or not, you are responding to this information moment to moment.

This input is what's guiding you through life. Your five senses provide data that helps you navigate and survive on the physical plane, while your sixth sense contributes input about how to live your life and fulfill your destiny as a spiritual being. The five senses guide the physical body, and the sixth sense guides the consciousness animating the body.

Given this, you can imagine how different life becomes once you are more consciously in touch with the sixth sense. Prior to a more complete opening of the sixth sense, you have only your five senses and conditioning to guide you, along with some access to the sixth sense. Your five senses and conditioning can keep you safe and alive and even make it possible to create an empire on earth, but they do little for the flowering of your spiritual being. Before the sixth sense opens up more fully, your spiritual being is quite latent, and the conditioned self, including the ego, is running the show.

This state is the one most of humanity is in, which isn't that different from animals, only more intelligent. However, such intelligence, as you can see by the condition of the world, is dangerous without spiritual development to balance and guide it. As a result, humanity has reached a crossroads. Your world is on the verge of destruction because human intelligence is receiving insufficient input from the more subtle senses, which inform the human about how to be the hero. Contact with the subtle world turns the human animal into the divine hero.

Without contact with your divine nature, the world is left to the ego and intellect. With the ego behind the wheel, the intellect ends up serving the ego's goals more than the intentions of the Whole, the Oneness. This is like a body whose cells don't know how to work together for the good of the whole. The ego is out for itself, and like cancer cells, the ego is killing off the very life forms that sustain it.

A higher intelligence than the ego and intellect must come into power within human consciousness for the world situation to change. That higher intelligence has always been activated within a small percentage of people and activated somewhat within a larger percentage than that. Now it's imperative that it become activated in many more people. This activation is being carried out on subtle dimensions and is affecting the gross physical, and the results are beginning to show. In more people than ever before in history, the hero is waking up.

This great awakening is an awakening of your inner goodness and every quality that is an expression of that. Every single one of those qualities—courage, love, peace, fortitude, patience, compassion, and wisdom—flows from your spiritual nature, not your human nature. It isn't human nature to be courageous or any of these other qualities. Something else within you is courageous, wise, peaceful, and loving. Without this mysterious, subtle dimension, humans would be animals.

Because the qualities of the hero stem from the subtle, spiritual dimension of your being, they can't be experienced by the five senses, nor are they a concept, but a spiritual reality. They are part of reality, although not part of tangible reality. And yet, they are more real than anything that can be sensed with the five senses and beyond anything that can be put into words.

What is most real and important in life is intangible, unmeasurable, and eternal. To deny this aspect of life because it can't be measured, put into words, or examined under a microscope is to disregard the most essential aspect of life: the spiritual dimension.

Perhaps the problem for some lies in the word "spiritual," since for so many, spirituality is equated with religion and its dogmatism and irrationalities. Those who like to see themselves as intelligent and rational often don't accept religion. So then, science becomes their religion, without realizing that science is narrow-minded in its own way. The limitation of science is its unwillingness to acknowledge the existence of anything that can't be tested, measured, and sensed with the five senses or current instrumentation.

Perhaps we need another word besides "spiritual," but we don't as yet have one. As a result, there will be those who will call the teachings in this book New Age spirituality and dismiss them. What would do this is the ego, looking to maintain its semblance of rationality, when in reality the ego is the epitome of irrationality.

It isn't rational to disregard the intangible matrix that lies behind and gives life to all of existence just because this matrix can't be proven to exist. It isn't something science can measure or understand, but that doesn't mean it is nonexistent or imaginary. What is most important and real is dismissed by much of science. That isn't rational. That's the ego running the intellect, and the ego is as irrational when it is controlling the intellect as when it isn't using the intellect at all.

So much can be accomplished when the hero uses the intellect instead of the ego. Then wisdom, creativity, sensitivity to the Whole, and vision can inform the intellect. Without these, the intellect becomes corrupted—the servant of a dark master. The intellect, itself, is neither good nor bad, moral nor immoral. It's only what is using it that makes it so.

What is this mysterious "thing" that can use the intellect wisely and for the good of all? It is the real you, which is the same you in each and every one of you. The goodness that each of you is, is the same goodness—God-ness—looking out of everyone's eyes and animating everyone's body. One thing—one consciousness—is moving life forward through you.

The catch is that this one consciousness decided to give itself a challenge by disguising the Oneness. Through genetic programming, you have been given an ego that makes you feel separate from and in competition with each other. The Oneness created the ego and the human to be just as it is, including its capacity to discover that it isn't really the ego or human at all!

So here you are, either just discovering this idea or already believing or not believing this. However, you either *know* this truth or you don't. It might be that believing this takes you to knowing it, but a belief alone cannot confer this knowing.

To know this truth is a gift of your evolution. It comes with Grace. You are given this knowing when it is time for you to know it. All of your life, and throughout all your lifetimes, you've been given the experiences, understanding, and inner qualities you have needed to evolve to the point when you would discover the truth about reality and who you are. It is your destiny to know this.

Because the hero knows who he is on a deep level, he has gained access to the qualities of the divine self and lives in alignment with those qualities. Through many experiences with life, he tried on many beliefs until he found ones that told the truth about reality, ones that provided an accurate map and led to happiness.

Let's take a look at some of the beliefs the hero came to believe along the way that helped him become the hero. An important one was just mentioned: You are given what you need to evolve. The hero discovered that, at every turn, no matter how challenging, he was given the inner and outer resources, assistance, opportunities, ideas, inspiration, wisdom, and motivation he needed to overcome any challenge and grow stronger as a result.

The hero came to recognize that every challenge was designed for his growth and had within it the potential for a successful outcome—and that it was up to him to make it successful. The hero understood that the measure of success was whether he became wiser, more compassionate, more skillful, and a better human being.

The belief that every experience is designed especially for you, for your growth, is a powerful reframing of the way the ego generally sees reality. And it is the truth. Seeing this about life allows you to make the most of every situation and to maintain a positive attitude throughout. With this perspective, there can be little suffering even under quite difficult circumstances.

Your attitude toward a challenge determines your experience of it and how difficult it will be for you. Some people sail through difficulties that break others. How you fare during tough times depends mostly on your attitude. It is that important. Beliefs are important because one's attitude is grounded in beliefs. They determine your attitude.

When you believe an experience is designed for you, you see it as good, even if it's difficult. To the hero, challenges aren't defined as bad or even difficult necessarily, and scary stories that would undermine the hero's courage aren't told. "It is all good" is the hero's mantra, and so he embraces the challenges he's been given. That acceptance grants the hero access to the other qualities of the divine self needed to navigate the challenge, such as courage and equanimity.

Your beliefs determine whether you will experience some challenge, or life in general, as bad or good, unsupportive or benevolent. Only the ego would define anything as bad, so if you are caught in that duality, you are identified with your ego. From the perspective of your divine self, all is truly good — there is no duality. The problem with the ego's perspective is that if you hold a negative story or belief about life, you will experience life as you believe it to be. Then accessing the good in an experience and the inner strengths you need to get you through it will be much more difficult.

Believing that your experiences are designed for your growth wouldn't do any good if this weren't also the truth. If challenges didn't actually develop your strengths and wisdom, then simply believing that wouldn't make it so. Beliefs can't change reality, even though they change one's experience of it. To be helpful, beliefs have to reflect reality accurately. The ego tries to change reality with its faulty beliefs — its *shoulds* and *coulds* — while the hero doesn't bother with beliefs that aren't true. He knows that only the ones that stand up to experience and match reality work and are useful.

The hero knows when life is working by how he feels, and he uses his feelings as guideposts. This brings us to another belief the hero has found useful: Follow your Heart, your bliss. He's discovered that life does come with a manual of sorts, and that manual is the Heart. It tells you how to live your life. The way the Heart communicates this is through certain feelings produced by the Heart.

The feelings the hero follows are not the same as emotions, which are byproducts of the ego and its negative thoughts. The Heart's feelings, such as joy and peace, are not feelings in the way that sadness and anger are. Joy, peace, love, compassion, delight, awe, gratitude, and contentment don't come from the ego but from the divine self, which is guiding you. In every moment, you are being guided by intuitions from the subtle realm and also by these feelings that come from the Heart. The Heart's feelings are less subtle than intuitions but more subtle than the emotions of the conditioned self.

Not feeding and acting out the usual emotions takes discipline, inner strength, and maturity. It's not easy to resist the path of least resistance, but the hero has discovered that it must be resisted. He's learned that negative emotions interfere with his goals of happiness, love, peace, and self-mastery. These goals come first over the temporary relief of releasing emotions thoughtlessly.

The hero follows the higher feelings of the divine self instead. When he does that, life goes well, while indulging emotions causes all kinds of troubles. The hero has learned to choose his path wisely. He chooses a path that may require discipline but takes him where he wants to go.

The hero goes where he wants to go. That may sound obvious, but many people don't go where they want to go but where they think they *should* go. Some people believe they have to do certain things whether they want to or not. This way of thinking might apply to brushing your teeth and eating well, but living your life a certain way because you think you have to or should is no way to live.

The hero knows this and makes choices that lead to being happy. He follows his bliss. And that is as it's meant to be. You are meant to be happy, so naturally the way to happiness is to do what makes you happy! When bliss is the path, then bliss is the result.

Shoulds and *can'ts* are what usually interfere with following one's bliss. These words point in the wrong direction, and yet they are so prevalent in the vocabulary of the thought-stream. Does this mean that the ego is out to make people unhappy? Not really. It's just that the ego doesn't know about happiness. It was built for safety, and safety and happiness are different goals, although not necessarily mutually exclusive.

If you listen only to the ego, you will probably gain safety, but you are likely to lose happiness. If you listen to the Heart, you will have both. Your divine self has every intention of keeping you safe, unless it has purposefully designed the opposite experience for you, in which case, you can't do anything to avoid that challenge anyway. Regardless, even within any unsafe situation, you are safe, since you are given every resource you need to handle it and grow from it, as long as you don't fall prey to the ego's negativity and fear.

The hero trusts the Heart more than the mind. He follows the Heart's guidance even when doing so doesn't make sense to the mind. What makes sense to the mind is whatever is assumed to bring greater safety, security, comfort, wealth, recognition, pleasure, or power. This leaves out a lot of valuable things! What about love, peace, creativity, fun, fulfillment, growth, wisdom, compassion, patience, inner strength—all of the things that are developed by challenges and valued by the divine self?

There are times when safety, security, pleasure, wealth, and other things the ego values must be sacrificed for what is of true value. If you seem to be being asked by life to sacrifice something, try to focus on what you might be gaining instead. Life is so benevolent that there is no time when you are asked to sacrifice in which you don't also gain. Every sacrifice or loss has within it a gain or win, if not immediately, then farther down the road. The hero looks to what is gained, not what is lost.

This brings us to the next belief the hero has found helpful: Losses are only apparent and temporary. Everything is temporary. Few things could be said about life that are truer than this statement. The mind says, "No!" when things it wants go. But coming and going is the way of life. There can be no coming without going. If not, this world would be a very crowded place! Everything has a lifespan, and when that lifespan is over, something else comes into being to take its place.

This endless march of change is neither right nor wrong, good nor bad, as the mind likes to declare. It is simply as it is and therefore as it is meant to be. The hero has learned that declaring something good or bad, or right or wrong, is a waste of energy. The hero accepts the comings and goings of life gracefully. He has seen that arguing with life or wishing it to be otherwise does no good. Acceptance is the only rational response to the changeability of life.

That acceptance helps the hero access other qualities he needs to cope with the challenges involved in change. Because the mind is programmed to suffer in times of loss, it takes diligence to not indulge in the faulty perceptions and negative emotions that try to take hold. Without a willingness to accept a loss and acknowledge its rightness in the scheme of things, suffering prevails.

One faulty perception, so embedded in language that it is difficult to recognize, is the idea of loss. The word "loss" appears to be simply a description of reality, but it is actually a story. It depicts something that is no longer here as lost or a loss, giving the natural leaving of something a negative emotional spin. This is the ego's point of view and only half the picture, since something is also coming to fill the vacuum.

Language is quite insidious this way. More often than not, it perpetuates the egoic point of view. This is one reason many spiritual traditions have included silence as a spiritual practice. Being silent helps you disengage from language and therefore the usual way of perceiving things. When language stops, you cease parsing the world into dualities, such as good and bad, and you can more easily disengage from feelings and preferences, all of which lead to resisting life as it is.

With every feeling you have, you are saying yes to something and no to something else. The same is true with preferences and desires. Language such as "good" and "bad" and "I like" and "I don't like" divides the world into what you want and don't want. Then when life shows up in a way you don't like, you suffer. By wanting life to look a certain way, you cause your own suffering. The hero has seen how such dualities and desires create suffering and how suffering wouldn't exist without them.

All suffering comes from the thought-stream, and we could just as well say from language. This is why the hero detaches himself from the thought-stream as much as possible and limits conversation, especially of an egoic nature. This may sound radical, but he's discovered that if you want to "be in the world but not of it," some silence is necessary, since language draws you into the misperceptions created by language.

Those misperceptions are the faulty map, and the hero knows that the faulty map leads to suffering and away from the treasure at his core. Importantly, he sees that there's a choice to be made: to agree with the world's misperceptions by allowing language to determine his perceptions or to question the misperceptions embedded in language.

The kingpin of language is the word "I." The hero doesn't believe what comes after that word. Those definitions attempt to put him into a box, to make him into a thing, when his true self is closer to being nothing than to being a thing. The hero knows his no-thing-ness, while most others do not. While language maintains the sense of people being things, or distinct entities, the hero knows that the truth is far from that. He experiences the spacious, wide-open vastness of his being and knows that he and life are far more mysterious than the mind's assumptions.

Everything is interconnected and interdependent and made of the same stuff: consciousness. All of the forms of life collectively are like the cells that make up your body. Each cell has a purpose and is intelligent, but its life is dependent on the vitality of the whole body. If one cell ceases to do its part or goes rogue, the whole body is affected. Every cell matters. That cell may not be consciously aware of its role within the whole, but its marching orders are embedded in its DNA, and so it knows what it needs to do to be what it's meant to be. You are a cell in the greater body of humankind and the universe. This is not a metaphor.

The hero doesn't believe the "I" portrayed by the thought-stream. He knows he isn't separate from the Whole, nor insignificant to it. He knows this from experience because he is attuned to the subtle world beyond the five senses, which has revealed this wholeness and interconnectedness to him.

This is the same Oneness experienced by mystics throughout time. The Oneness is not hidden for those whose more subtle senses are open. So although a belief in Oneness may be helpful in the beginning stages of realizing this truth, Oneness is not a belief, but an experience that is beyond the mind's ability to grasp.

The truth about reality can only be experienced by moving out of the mind. The mind doesn't believe in a greater reality beyond its illusory mental reality, and the mind doesn't and cannot know reality. Something else can, though, and that is the awakening hero in every person. At a certain point in everyone's evolution, something wakes up inside that is willing to question the mind and what it says about reality. This mysterious something—the real you—is no doubt either already awake or awakening in you.

The hero has discovered something very important about this Oneness: Love is the stuff it is made of—consciousness *is* love. Love is the most powerful force in the universe, and creation is an expression of this love. The Father is this love and represents the intelligence that seeded this and every other universe and continues to guide creation lovingly. No matter how absent love may seem within human endeavors, it remains ever-present, immutable, and unstoppable. It is the constant that underlies and fuels the universe. And it is the ever-available resource you've been given to support you on this human journey.

In myths and legends, the hero often comes into possession of a magical sword or some other magical item to get him through the direst of times. Love is that sword. It vanquishes evil, mends hearts, pierces through illusion, and redeems the hero. Love is also the magical harp or trumpet that summons supernatural forces to assist the hero. And love is the genie that bestows all wishes. Love is the magic each of you has been given to help you on your way.

The hero learned about love by noticing how life works or doesn't work:

The hero noticed that when he was kind, life worked, and when he wasn't kind, life didn't work.

The hero noticed that whenever he gave something or someone his full attention, love flowed, and then he was happy and others were happy.

The hero noticed that love is receptive and patient, and when he was receptive and patient, others loved him and came to his aid.

The hero noticed that when he did what he loved doing, he was happy and he became better at it easily.

The hero noticed that when he was loving and happy, others were attracted to him and wanted to be around him and be good to him.

The hero noticed that when he behaved lovingly, he was happy, and when he didn't behave lovingly, he wasn't happy.

The hero noticed that when he forgave others, he stopped suffering and was able to move on and love again.

The hero also noticed that when he forgave himself, he was able to move on and love himself again.

The hero noticed that giving love felt better than receiving it.

The hero noticed that he could choose to love anyone or anything, and then love would flow from him. He learned there was a fountain of love available within himself, which never went dry. And so he realized that feeling loving and therefore feeling happy was always in his power.

The hero noticed that if he let love, excitement, and joy lead him, he would be happy and find his way to greater love, peace, and happiness. He discovered that love is both the path and the reward of following the path.

The hero had to conclude that there was something very special about love, perhaps more special than anything else. So he aligned himself with love. The more he acted in accordance with love, the happier he became and the better his life worked out. Love works magic!

Love is not a belief but the greatest truth about reality. However, if you believe the opposite of this truth, you will have the opposite experience. For instance, if you believe that nothing like love or a higher intelligence is behind life, you will be guided by the mind, since that is humanity's default state. Then you will have the ego's experience of life, which is fear, competition, and lack, and discovering the power of love will be more difficult.

Nevertheless, it is only a matter of time before you would catch on to the magic of love. No one can *not* discover this not-very-hidden secret. Life is designed so that you will discover this truth. At every turn, life teaches you love. You only have to notice, like the hero, what life is teaching you.

CHAPTER 8

The Hero's Destiny

Everyone has a destiny. Every soul, before coming into life, resolves to accomplish certain goals and lessons. This curriculum is a person's destiny. The specifics of how that curriculum will play out are not set prior to birth but depend to some degree on free will, including the free will of others. More important than free will in determining the specifics are the actions taken by spiritual forces, whose function it is to create circumstances conducive to the soul's learning.

Spiritual forces shape this curriculum by bringing people opportunities, experiences, events, ideas, and other people and by inspiring and motivating them. Within these circumstances, a person makes choices. However, free will by no means determines what someone will encounter in life or even what he or she will be moved to do. The pull of one's destiny is far more compelling than the will of the ego and the conditioned self.

Within this destiny are certain destiny points, which are experiences chosen prior to life that shape one's life in some significant way. These destiny points might be a health crisis, meeting someone important, an innovative idea, a career opportunity, a spiritual experience, a near-death experience, the loss of a child, a financial windfall, or some other life-changing event.

These destiny points are unavoidable and meant to be transformative, so they must be accepted, surrendered to, and taken advantage of. The ego might feel victimized by the more challenging experiences, but that would make it hard to make the most of these important turning points.

In between these destiny points, life continues to be a dance between a person's free will and divine will, which is administered by spiritual forces. In any moment, a person's choices are either aligned with the ego or the divine self. Either way, the person is likely to be learning something, although he or she might not be fulfilling his or her destiny.

If someone is not learning what the soul intends, spiritual forces might intervene to try to shake that person out of a particular mindset or steer that person in another direction. This is often accomplished through some sort of crisis or challenge, such as an illness, a job loss, a divorce, or financial difficulties, which spiritual forces are capable of arranging.

Spiritual forces are involved in guiding and shaping everyone's life, whether a person is aware of these forces or not. When people are aware of and open to them, or at least believe they exist, spiritual forces can have more of a positive influence. Intuitions are one of the ways these forces are able to affect people who are open to the more subtle realms. But intuitions are by no means the only way spiritual forces have to guide and shape people's lives.

For clarity, it might be important to define what I mean by spiritual forces. Many call these forces *beings,* but that word is a bit misleading. It implies that spiritual forces are more similar to human beings than they are. How they are alike is that most have had human lifetimes, so they understand the human condition. But that doesn't mean they are entities with personalities and a personal will. And that's a big difference.

The spiritual forces I'm referring to have no personal will or personal agenda but work on behalf of the One. They have no judgments and wish you only the best, if it could even be called wishing. The problem with language is that, because spiritual forces can't be fully known to you or comprehended by the mind, language doesn't exist to describe this form of life.

Even the words "form of life" imply a form, when none exists. To call them "forces" is more accurate than any word that implies a form. Although spiritual forces can take on a form and a personality of sorts to interact with those who are able to be aware of them, that form doesn't represent them in the least. They are not representable, so little can be said about them.

What can be said about them is that they are forces for good in everyone's life. They carry out the workings and evolution of the One. They are servants who serve life. ("Servants" is another one of those misleading words.) The functions of these forces are very specifically defined. There are spiritual forces who guide humans and each of the other kingdoms: animal, plant, and mineral. The efficiency, perfection, and intelligence of the One is unfathomable.

The hero moves in alignment with this perfection and, with every breath, offers praise to it. She is supremely happy as a result. When one realizes this perfection on a deep level, the only possible response is gratitude, awe, and devotion. This is, in essence, how the hero lives each moment. What I'm describing is the enlightened human being, the most developed expression of the hero. This is every person's ultimate destiny. Arriving at the realization of this perfection is the purpose of all of your incarnations.

Some of how spiritual forces affect humanity will have to remain a mystery, since there aren't words to describe how this works. But the more obvious ways can be described. The most apparent way they affect you is through your intuition. However, the effectiveness of that method depends on how developed one's intuition is and how much it is listened to.

Variations in the development of intuition can, in part, explain why some people's lives run more smoothly than others. Some appear to be blessed with a kind of grace or protection that follows them about. Although such individuals may seem to be living a charmed life, such help and shielding are available to anyone who is tuned in to the subtle realms. This attunement can be developed, but a person has to choose to cultivate it. For those who don't believe that subtle realms exist, that is the catch.

Another of the more obvious ways spiritual forces can influence you and circumstances is by speaking to you mentally. This mental communication is experienced as a distinct inner voice, with a tonality and feel that's different from your own thoughts.

This kind of communication usually occurs to help someone avoid an accident, although there are those, such as this author, who are given mental messages on a regular basis for the purpose of serving humanity. When this mental communication comes as a warning, the message is usually brief and to the point: "Don't go there!" "Look left!" "Stop!" "Be careful."

Spiritual forces also can affect you and circumstances by appearing to you as an angel, a light being, or a person who delivers a message or stops you from doing something you were about to do. This kind of intervention is most common during critical events and at the end of life, when spiritual forces often appear to the one dying and to their loved ones to convey comforting messages and help with that transition.

Spiritual forces regularly save people from experiences they aren't meant to have. People find themselves in such situations usually because of someone else's poor choice. When accidents involve those who either don't need that experience for their growth or whose growth would be hindered by that experience, spiritual forces intervene to protect those individuals. You can probably think of times in your own life when you had close calls or brushes with death, which no doubt involved spiritual forces coming to your rescue. At the time, you might even have been aware of those forces.

The reason spiritual forces don't intervene more often to protect people is that most of the time people are having the experience they're meant to have, either because they created it and therefore need to learn from that choice or because that experience is part of their destiny. Another reason spiritual forces might not intervene is out of respect for your free will. They respect your right to choose and learn from your choices and understand that this choice-making process is integral to evolution.

The hero also realizes that progressing in life means making so-called mistakes and that, in fact, there is no such thing. A mistake is just a concept, a story. "I made a mistake" is not the truth but a particular viewpoint—that of the ego. Because the hero understands the role of so-called mistakes, she accepts them as part of life. She doesn't expect to be perfect, nor does she expect life to be easy and without challenges. She is realistic and sees reality as it is.

Implied in the word "mistake" is that something went wrong or happened that shouldn't have happened, which is a false assumption. Anything that happened needed to happen, or it wouldn't have happened. It needed to happen to show you something, perhaps to teach you something about some choice. Everything serves a purpose and therefore cannot be a mistake. The only mistake, if you could call it that, would be to not learn from some experience. But that would be impossible anyway.

Certain choices may have an undesirable outcome, but that doesn't make them a mistake. That undesirable outcome inevitably points you in a new direction, which is the purpose of that so-called mistake. Course corrections are constantly being made in life as a result of so-called mistakes. This is how people learn to navigate life and how they learn what works. There's no other way, really. No one is born knowing how to play this game of life; it has to be learned.

You learn by doing, discovering something, and making another choice. Everyone is playing it by ear in life.

To the hero, life is a grand game that, by definition, must include both winning and losing. She knows you can't have one without the other. What would winning be without sometimes losing? It makes winning all the sweeter, and winning soothes the wounds of all prior losses. As with any game, winning and losing make the game of life fun. The hero realizes this and embraces both winning and losing. She also realizes that every win and every loss is only temporary.

The hero doesn't take winning or losing personally. Because she understands she isn't responsible for or in control of all aspects of the game, she doesn't take credit or blame for the way things go. Recognizing that she is but one small player in the game of life, the hero faces each circumstance with courage and curiosity and does her best.

In the game of life, as in all games, you never know how things are going to turn out. The hero knows she doesn't know, and she doesn't pretend to know, but she maintains a positive outlook anyway.

Remaining optimistic in the midst of not knowing while not bolstering oneself by pretending to know is no small accomplishment. The ego gains courage from pretending to know the outcome and then becomes discouraged when things turn out differently. The hero, on the other hand, gains courage from knowing that whatever the outcome is, it is good. So she is never disappointed by life. This is how she lives out her destiny, with courage, optimism, and gratitude for life.

The hero knows that she has a destiny and that, as part of that destiny, both gifts and challenges are given to her "by the gods." Gifts and challenges come as one package: Just as you can't have wins without losses, you can't have gifts without challenges. The gifts are bestowed to overcome the challenges, and the challenges are delivered to develop the gifts. The hero is willing to accept both unquestioningly. What would be the point of arguing with the elegance of this design?

And yet, the ego holds debates with life: "Why did you do this to me? How could you do this to me? Why me?" The ego is angry with life, blames life, and pleads with life—all irrational acts, which only serve to make one the unhappy victim.

To the ego, life is cruel. But the hero holds no such imagination or story. Life is what it is, and the hero doesn't tell a discouraging story or one that causes her to feel negatively about herself or about life. This difference makes all the difference and is essentially what makes the hero a hero.

The hero doesn't actually know her destiny, only that she has one and that it's discovered by noticing what life is bringing *now*, in this moment, and *now* in this moment. One's destiny is both the destiny points and everything in between, because every choice in every ordinary moment also affects and potentially contributes to one's destiny.

The destiny points are not in the hero's control, but her moment-to-moment *experience* of life is. The hero knows that the only thing she can control is her experience of life by managing her thoughts and attitudes. The rest, the hero leaves to the Father. What she can affect, she affects; and what she cannot affect, she leaves to the Father. She can affect her experience of life and, in that, to some extent affect life. But the hero doesn't pretend she can control the perfect unfolding of life. And why would she even want to?

Once the perfection is seen, the need for control falls away, and with it, the hero tumbles into life and lets life carry her where it will. She observes where life is flowing and goes with it. The flow is life happening perfectly, as it is meant to. The hero's only job is to say yes to it. That is how the hero creates with life. She creates what life wants her to create. She is able to do this because she's attuned to the flow and knows what life wants.

Life wants something different for each person, which is why you have to pay attention to the moment you are given. It is how you discover what life wants of you personally. Life has a plan for you, which you discover by paying attention to what's coming out of the flow now, and now, and now.

The ego also has a plan for you, and so it tries to take you out of the flow to get you to follow its plan. It's the standard, one-size-fits-all plan. This plan works some of the time, but it can't fulfill you like the plan that is specifically designed for you.

Your destiny is something your soul chose before you were born. It was chosen lovingly and with great care:

It might be a destiny that involves doing something in the world, like being a pianist, a teacher, or a politician.

Or your destiny might involve cultivating a way of being: being more loving, being more courageous, being more patient, or being more responsible.

Some have a destiny to develop their mind or to learn about something and possibly share that learning.

Many have a destiny that shapes their character. They might be learning to be less selfish or less ego-driven. Or they might just be finding out what it's like to be very selfish and ego-driven.

Others have a destiny that involves developing a talent or skill, in which case, they might not yet shine at that talent or skill, but they are fulfilled by it anyway because they feel moved to pursue it.

Still others have a destiny to serve, and the way they do that might not be important.

As you can see from this list, one's destiny might not even seem like a destiny. Nevertheless, no one's destiny is more important than anyone else's. Each destiny serves the Whole and is designed to do that. Although it might appear that someone has a very fortunate destiny while someone else does not, to each soul, fulfilling the chosen destiny is what's important.

You know when you are fulfilling your destiny by how you feel. When you're fulfilling it, you are naturally happy, unless you believe you should be doing something else. This natural happiness can be diminished if you think your life should look different than it does, perhaps more glamorous or interesting. But that would be the ego's desire, not your soul's.

Because the ego wants certain things, such as power, money, and prestige, people often feel that accomplishments that don't bring these benefits are lesser, when there is potentially as much fulfillment in those accomplishments for that person as in so-called greater accomplishments. If the ego had its way, everyone would be a rock star, the president of the United States, or a CEO—and what kind of a world would that be!

The Perfection has prescribed the perfect role for everyone. In the scheme of many, many lifetimes, everyone gets to try out the full range of roles. The Perfection is ultimately evenhanded and wise.

When you reach the end of your lifetimes on earth, you realize that all along you've been playing all the roles, as you come to recognize yourself as the One in everyone. You see that there never actually was a *you* separate from anything. One Being is doing it all, and you are that. Any injustices you perceived about life were from the perspective of the *you* that you thought you were. But if, in truth, you are both the one experiencing an injustice and meting it out, where is the injustice?

The hero knows she has a destiny, a place in the Whole, and she knows what that place is by paying attention to her interior world. This is not the world of thoughts and feelings, as you might assume, but a subtler world that communicates information and instructions through intuitions, drives, inspiration, joy, peace, and excitement. The hero knows that if she's too involved in the usual thoughts and feelings, she may miss these more subtle instructions that reveal to her how to move moment to moment.

This subtle world can be difficult to decipher at times. It takes practice to hear one's intuition, and it takes trust to follow it. Both of these need time to develop. In the meantime, the awakening hero asks spiritual forces for assistance in knowing what is true, how to move, and how to be in her life. She asks for healing, guidance, protection, and help from them, knowing that she'll receive these things as needed. Then she lets go and trusts that she'll know what she needs to know when she needs to know it.

Such prayers for assistance make it possible to relax into life, into the moment. They help you feel that all is well, which is the truth. They counteract the sense that comes from the ego that you have to struggle and strive just to exist. Nothing could be farther from the truth.

The ego creates a sense of life being a problem and something to be feared. This activates the negative mind and produces tension, stress, and negative emotions. This state of arousal may have been useful at some point in humanity's evolution, but now it is more problematic than helpful.

Relaxation is a much more functional and productive state and also enables you to be in touch with the subtle world that supports the physical world. All of life is informed and sustained by the subtle world, and human beings are no exception. They, like everything else, are grounded in and receive their energy and their very life from the subtle realm.

This is the realm that the greater Intelligence uses to communicate with the physical realm to maintain and manage it. When you attune to the subtle realm, you are attuning to this greater Intelligence and the design it has for you. Just as a seed carries the instructions for the plant, the subtle realm carries the instructions for every living thing. It is the blueprint for all of life.

When you are relaxed, you are more able to sense this subtle realm than when you are tense, because tension means you are identified with the thoughts and emotions that belong to the ego. Doing things that allow you to relax will therefore give you access to this subtle realm.

There are many things that promote relaxation. Prayer is one of them. In prayer, you hand over, or surrender, your so-called problems, fears, and concerns to a "higher power." This is very healing. Doing this frees you from the ego's problems, fears, and concerns. They truly are just the ego's and not real in any way.

As believable as your problems or fears may seem, they still don't exist. This may seem like a ridiculous claim, but that would be your programming speaking. Naturally the ego, which is the generator of problems and fears, can't see that these are imaginary. But something wiser can. What is it that can see that a fear is not based in reality, in the here and now? What is it that can evaluate the veracity of your thoughts? That is who you really are.

In prayer, you surrender your ego's perspective. In doing so, what remains is reality. When you drop your fears and concerns, you drop into the simple here and now. Within that are all the answers you will ever need for how to live your life. Just as a child might hand over a torn picture to her mother for mending, you hand over your broken thoughts and feelings to the Father, and they're made right. The feeling of relaxation is how you know they've been made right.

Passing on a problem to someone else is such a relief, especially when you know that problem is something that person can handle easily. Prayer is like that: You give your problem to a higher power to handle it for you. The truth is that the problem never did exist and the higher power has been handling life perfectly all along. But to relax your ego and mind, participating in this ritual of prayer can be very helpful.

You could say that what relaxes is the animal part of you, which is fear-based. It needs to be soothed somehow so that it doesn't sabotage your life. It isn't wise, and it's churning out fearful, stress-producing, and nonproductive thoughts.

Prayer is one way to calm "the beast" within. Even if there were no spiritual forces to answer your prayers, praying would be healing for the simple reason that it calms your brain's limbic system and helps you become present, assuming you believe in prayer.

There's another reason to believe in the power of prayer: Prayer gives you the confidence that, with help, you *can* overcome the ego's fears and negativity. One of the ways the ego stays in control is by convincing you that it is powerful. This belief, like so many others, is a self-fulfilling prophecy, as it dis-courages you and keeps you from accessing the strengths of the hero. Prayer is a way to regain access to those strengths.

Prayer works for another reason: Spiritual forces do exist! And they exist to serve you. When they see that you want help in combatting fears and other negativity, they provide it, even though you might not be aware of it. Clearing negativity is one of their jobs, but they won't necessarily do that unless asked.

What is the best way to pray? The sincerity of the prayer is more important than the specific words. Spiritual forces respond most strongly to fervent supplications. However, that doesn't mean you will get whatever you ask for just because you pray for it (which you've probably noticed). Life doesn't necessarily give people want they want, because it has its own plan and reasons for providing or not providing what it does.

What you can be sure of is that you will get the help you need for dealing with whatever you are struggling with. That help may come in the form of inner strength, a book, an important idea or insight, a shift in attitude, help from a friend, or benefits in other areas of your life to ease your circumstances.

It's always best to avoid praying for anything specific, such as more money, a relationship, or even improved health. These aspects of your life are the way they are for a reason, and they will change in their own time. Often a particular lesson has to be learned, an understanding has to be arrived at, a different choice has to be made, or a character trait needs to be developed before the challenges in a particular area disappear.

There's a time for everything, and when the time for what you are experiencing has passed, it will be time for something else. Everyone experiences cycles around finances, relationships, health, and career. You are always having the right experience, and your experience is continually changing as a result of either changing circumstances or your evolving understanding.

The desires that run through your thought-stream, which you might be tempted to pray for, don't represent what is best for you, even if they seem to. People who are sick are sure they would be better off well, and most who are single are sure they would be better off in a relationship. But that isn't necessarily true. The ego doesn't see the whole picture or the long-range picture. It doesn't see the benefits in being sick or single, or in other challenges. That which is living your life knows much better than the ego what is best for you.

There are much better prayers to pray than ones that ask for some desire to be met. Praying for help in maintaining a positive attitude in the midst of some difficulty is an especially good prayer. Here are some others:

Help me see this situation in a new light.

Help me learn what I need to learn from this.

Help me know the truth about this situation.

Help me know what's best to do for all concerned.

Give me the strength to stay positive and do what I need to do now.

Help me be my best self.

I'm ready and willing to receive any healing, insight, and help with this.

Please help clear any negativity that's in my environment and protect me from negativity as I go out into the world.

These are the types of prayers that are always answered. These are also the things that are important to ask for so that you receive the most benefit possible from spiritual forces.

You can never pray too often. One of the mistakes people make is they think they don't need to ask a second time for something. But you do. You need to ask again and again for as long as you need to. Here's why: If you get caught in negative thoughts and feelings, spiritual forces regard that as you choosing those thoughts, since you aren't choosing to disregard them. Because spiritual forces respect your free will, they won't interfere with your choice to think those thoughts. So if you want help with any negative thoughts and feelings, you have to ask for help whenever you need it.

When you catch yourself contracted and immersed in negative thoughts and feelings, that's the time to pray for help in shifting your consciousness. Do this diligently each time you are caught in the mind's lies, and you will see a difference. It will become increasingly easy to not get caught or not stay caught.

Prayer works. It is one of the most important tools of the awakening hero. The fully awakened hero's life *is* a prayer: "Thank you for this perfection and all the help you continually bestow upon me. Thank you for this love and bounty, which I gladly receive so that I may be a lamp of love and service in the world."

Prayer brings you into the hero's world, which is beautiful and abundant. Then you find yourself praying, not for yourself as much as for all of humanity, that they might discover what you have discovered: Life is good.

CHAPTER 9

The Hero's Lifestyle

Just as those who are ego-driven create a lifestyle around what makes the ego happy, the hero creates a lifestyle around what makes him happy. From the outside, these lifestyles may not appear that different, but they are likely to be lived quite differently.

There are two kinds of happiness: the kind that comes and goes relatively quickly when you get what you want and the kind that is an ever-present quality of reality and the result of living in reality. Ego-driven people and the hero experience both kinds of happiness but to different degrees. Since the same things make people happy, this isn't surprising. Everyone likes ice cream, colorful sunsets, happy babies, hot showers, winning, achieving, acquiring, creating, and loving, to name just a few of the joys of being human.

What makes you happy doesn't change when you become the hero. You still enjoy all the things you ever did and many more—and you appreciate them much more. What changes is that you no longer need the more egoic pleasures and achievements to be happy. You can be happy even if you don't succeed at something, even if you don't have access to a hot shower or your favorite foods, and even if you aren't successful, rich, or good looking in other people's eyes. In other words, you can be happy even if you don't have the things the ego holds dear and necessary for happiness.

The ego and the hero have very different values, needs, desires, and perceptions, and these result in very different ways of being in the world:

> *The ego believes it needs certain things to be happy, and the hero is just happy.*

> *The ego needs to be someone, and the hero just needs to be.*

> *The ego foregoes being happy now for a promise of happiness in the future, while the hero does what makes him happy now.*

> *The ego wants, and the hero finds satisfaction in what he has.*

> *The ego believes happiness comes from having and getting, while the hero knows the true source of happiness.*

The kind of happiness the ego seeks is different than the hero's natural happiness. The ego seeks the thrill of getting what it wants: the excitement of having a new car, the sense of specialness in being promoted or recognized, the ecstasy of a promising relationship, the superiority of looking good, the satiety of indulgence, the self-satisfaction of having money, and the pride in winning.

Unfortunately, the journey to the ego's goals is often spoiled by the suffering involved in wanting something and not having it. Because the ego struggles so much with being happy in between achieving its goals, attaining a goal brings a sudden and often short-lived rush of happiness—and great relief. The relief the ego feels when it finally gets what it wants is like the relaxation of a tightly held muscle. Finally, the pain of wanting is over! This is one kind of happiness. Most people seem to live for these moments, while pushing, striving, and sleepwalking through the rest of their lives.

The hero also enjoys the things the ego enjoys, but without the rush, because the hero doesn't give personal meaning to attaining these things, as the ego does. When the ego gets what it wants, it gleefully declares: "Now everyone will look up to me. Now I'm a winner. Now my life is finally going the way I want it to. Now I'll finally be happy!" What the ego attains is always attached to a larger story about what that will mean personally. The ego pumps up its winning moments with reasons why that achievement is more meaningful than it actually is.

With the ego, everything is always about *me*. The ego invests the things it wants with a magical ability to produce specialness, superiority, and happiness, even though those things don't have that power. In the end, the moment of happiness passes, like every other moment, with nothing remaining but a flimsy memory and most likely the old feelings of not being enough or having enough.

When the ego gets what it wants, its *belief* in the power of that to make it happy makes the ego very, very happy momentarily, until the ego discovers that that happiness isn't forever. Then the ego has to find another goal to achieve, mountain to climb, or thing to acquire so that it can then, once and for all, be happy. The thing that will make the ego happy forever is always just out of reach, around the next corner. Briefly attained and quickly lost, the ego's happiness is illusive but powerful while it lasts. This is the happiness most aspire to.

The kind of happiness that the hero knows is more subtle and ongoing. It isn't dependent on circumstances but on contact with reality and the hero's true nature. The source of lasting happiness is precisely this, and every other kind of happiness pales in comparison. When you have found what the hero has, everything else that can be gained in life is frosting on the cake but not necessary. There is an ultimate reward for living many, many lifetimes, and that reward is ongoing contentment with life just as it is.

This contentment is so much richer than that word implies, because within it is joy, wonder, gratitude, awe, and delight in life and in being alive. These divine feelings arise in the simplest and most ordinary moments, and to evoke them requires nothing more than your attention. When the hero gives his attention to the sunlight streaming in the window, for instance, he is flooded with the delight of that experience. When something as unimportant to the ego as sunlight can bring you joy, you know you have come Home.

Could anything be better than that joy? Not really. What the hero experiences as a result of being in contact with reality and his true nature is as fulfilling as any experience a human being can have. It is what people are searching for when they pursue the things the ego wants. But those things don't bring that same joy. The happiness that flows from deep contentment is qualitatively different from the happiness the ego enjoys when it gets what it wants.

This deeper, natural happiness is available in every moment, but it is often overlooked because it's more subtle than the rush and thrill of the other kind of happiness. Even so, it is actually richer and more fulfilling. It satisfies in a way that the ego's happiness does not. The ego's happiness is based on a fantasy, while this innate joy is the experience of reality. Whenever you touch deeply into reality, this joy is there. Being in reality is the ultimate reward, the ultimate happiness.

The hero's life and lifestyle are based on this deeper joy, just as the ego's life and lifestyle are based on its search for happiness through the acquisition of things, money, status, power, recognition, comfort, safety, and security.

The hero's life is also based on being, while the ego's is based on having and doing. And yet there is plenty of having and plenty of doing in the hero's life, but that having and doing are informed by being. The ego's doing, on the other hand, as well as what it seeks to have, are informed by the thought-stream. This difference creates very different lives and lifestyles:

The ego takes a job for security, while the hero takes a job aligned with his Heart.

The ego eats mostly for pleasure, while the hero eats mostly to sustain his body.

The ego struggles against responsibilities or is compulsively driven by them, while the hero stays balanced and naturally does what needs to be done when it needs to be done.

The ego associates with those who enhance the ego's sense of self and agree with its beliefs, while the hero associates with those who help him be who he is meant to be.

The ego serves only those who can benefit it, while the hero finds benefit in serving whomever is in front of him.

The ego pursues its goals, while the hero lets life take him where it wants him to go.

The ego has a plan for everything, while the hero has none and needs none.

The ego believes it knows where it's going, while the hero knows he doesn't know and doesn't need to know. The hero finds out where he is going when he gets there.

The ego has fun by indulging in pleasures, while the hero takes pleasure in everything.

The ego does things to get something, while the hero does things for the sake of doing them.

The ego gives to others to look good in other people's eyes, while the hero gives because he sees himself in the eyes of others.

The ego is addicted to stress and copes with it through escapism and overindulgences, while the hero doesn't create stress and is therefore always happy and at peace.

The ego fills the mind with beliefs and opinions, while the hero empties the mind, leaving it free to receive the truth.

The ego keeps a closed mind, while the hero keeps an open mind.

The ego uses the mind to try to control life, while the hero uses the intellect to free himself from the egoic mind.

The ego is at war with life, always on guard and ready for battle, while the hero trusts life and feels at one with it.

The ego works hard to shape life to its desires, while the hero desires what life wants and what it is already providing.

The ego wants for everything, while the hero wants for nothing.

To the ego, the hero looks like a fool, a dangerous fool. The hero's way of being in life is frightening to the ego. It doesn't want any part of being, flowing, letting things be, accepting life, or even loving life. That would give life too much control, and the ego believes it must be in control to be safe—as if it even can be!

To the ego, safety is foremost, above all else, because the ego deeply believes it isn't safe from life. This is one of the core lies that keeps the ego's illusory reality in place. But life *is* safe. Life *is* trustworthy. If you don't believe this, your life will remain in the hands of the ego, the programming.

The programming causes you to believe you aren't safe when you are. People write science fiction movies and books about computers taking over the world. Well, in a sense, they already have, and most people aren't aware of it: The programming has taken people over, usurped their God-given power to choose. It tells you, "Do this, do that, go here, not there," and you listen because you believe you won't be safe if you don't. The programming controls you through fear.

How is this not like a dictatorship, except that you willingly give your power to the programming? Most people never question the voice in their head. They don't question it because they are programmed not to and because it seems like their own voice. It seems like *you* are telling *you* what to do, but it is *not* you.

Very clever, don't you think? And isn't it also clever to give the voice a benign and all-knowing tone? A benign, all-knowing dictator—just what everyone wants! This is how the ego's illusory world is kept in place. So who is the *you* who is able to see through the scam, who can see the truth right now? That is the real you. Even more clever!

The hero has seen through the scam, and he's no longer buying it. Seeing this gave him the courage to follow his Heart instead of the thought-stream. So he stopped doing some of the things he was doing out of fear and started doing what he is naturally drawn to doing, what feels right to do. He discovered that what feels right to do actually works, makes him happy, and makes others happy. He discovered that he was right about life and the ego was wrong: Life is more than trustworthy; life is very, very good.

The mind can come up with a lot of arguments to support its perceptions and beliefs, but every one of them is based on these same faulty beliefs and perceptions. The ego's reasoning is circular. For instance, the ego believes that to be happy you have to strive to get what you want. But that's only true if you believe you will only be happy if you get what you want. In truth, striving isn't necessary to be happy, only to get what the ego wants. Furthermore, if you believe striving is necessary for happiness, then how will you ever find out that it isn't? You'll be too busy and too much in the ego's pocket to discover otherwise.

Another example of such a belief is the belief that the world is unsafe. And yet, "unsafe" is a concept, a story about life, which creates the inner experience of unsafe if you believe it. The ego's beliefs, like this one, only *feel* true; they aren't *actually* true. The ego's beliefs are a magic trick, which makes life seem as if it is as the ego claims it to be. If you remain in those beliefs, how will you discover otherwise?

The hero has the courage to question the ego's assumptions. As a result, he discovers the truth and has a different experience of life than most people, a happier and more peaceful one. Your beliefs create your experience of life. Change your beliefs, and your experience of life changes. That is the magic *you* have.

When your beliefs match reality, you stop suffering. The way to discover the beliefs that match reality is by questioning the beliefs that cause suffering. Once you see through the false beliefs at the root of your suffering, what is left are beliefs that match reality, ones that don't cause suffering. When you move out of the ego's convoluted, complicated, and confused world, life is simple: When your beliefs don't match reality, you suffer; when they do match reality, you don't suffer.

Life has a way of pointing you Home, but you have to pay attention in each moment to how your body feels when you think a thought. Does that thought contract you or relax and quiet you? Tension is an indication that you are believing something false, while relaxation indicates truth. Relaxation is a sign of being Home; tension is a sign of ensnarement in the ego's illusory world.

The hero creates a lifestyle using this simple guideline. It's his homing device, how he knows whether he is following his Heart or not. When he feels bad, he knows he isn't following his Heart, and when he feels at peace, he knows he is. Too simple, you say? Try it out. But, be forewarned, when you do venture to follow your Heart, you will come face to face with fear.

Fear is how the ego keeps the truth hidden and keeps you caught in the illusion. It is the ego's most powerful tool for maintaining the illusion. Fear is, itself, an illusion but a difficult one to see through because it has a bodily component. When it's believed, fear becomes a sensation in the body—and that *is* real.

The trick is to catch fear when it's only a thought, before it becomes an emotion. Once it becomes an emotion, more effort and fortitude will be needed to dismiss it and escape its influence. Once fear is felt in the body, you will have to sit with it quietly, investigate it, and discover the thoughts that gave birth to it. You'll have to walk yourself back to the origin of the fear and see that it's just a thought: an untrue, unverifiable assumption about the future.

Even if you do this investigation, the falseness of the fear might not be immediately apparent. Once a fear manifests in the body, the body thinks it is real, so you may have to convince the body otherwise. One way of counteracting the body's stress reaction is with positive statements that produce relaxation. These may be general calming statements, such as "All is well," or more specific statements designed to neutralize that particular fear. You have to try on some possibilities for yourself and see what works.

As you follow your Heart, you will also have to deal with other people's fears. Everyone's ego has the same fears about stepping outside the programming. So when you go against the *shoulds, coulds,* and *woulds* that everyone puts so much stock in, you will have to face not only your own fears, but everyone else's. You will have to find the courage to not be swayed by others and by any need for their approval. This is where many get stuck.

Many know their Heart and are in touch with the drive to fulfill it, but they can't bring themselves to do anything that would hurt or worry those close to them, particularly family members. This is an understandable concern and seems to come from love and compassion; however, underlying it is a fear of being ostracized. This fear is very primal, going back to your earliest roots, where survival depended on loyalty to one's tribe. Because this fear runs so deep, it continues to run many people unconsciously. Surely empathy is part of this concern for others, but it isn't the whole story.

More importantly, underlying the concern about hurting others is a misunderstanding: the belief that it is possible for you to hurt others. This may sound strange because it goes against conventional understanding, but it is impossible for you to hurt others. It is only possible for them to hurt themselves with their own negative beliefs and stories. Without a negative story, there's no possible way for them to suffer.

They might be arguing that you will never be happy, you'll be poor, they'll never see you, or you'll get hurt, all of which are unsubstantiated and likely untrue. Even if something they predicted were to happen, that would be the right experience for your growth. Following your Heart is not necessarily free of hardships or challenges. Or others might be believing that you are wrong, foolish, naive, silly, or crazy for doing what you want to do, which are judgments and also lies. These are the kinds of things that keep the programming in place: fears, judgments, and other lies. People keep each other enslaved in the programming.

Are you responsible for or in control of the beliefs or stories others have about you and therefore responsible for or in control of their feelings and their suffering? Not at all. How could you be? You are only responsible for the stories you tell yourself about yourself and about others. You didn't put those stories in their heads, and you can't remove them.

The best you can do is try to help your loved ones see things differently so that they don't suffer. If they won't or can't, then there is little else you can do but let them be the way they are, keep loving them, and hope they will do the same for you. In the end, you can only do so much to save people from their self-induced suffering.

Everyone has to discover the cause of their suffering themselves. It is this very inquiry into suffering that wakes people up. Until then, obeying their programming is the right experience for them. Everyone is always having the right experience, whether they are following their Heart or not, for every experience eventually leads to the Heart, although some journeys are longer and more rugged than others.

How long it takes to wake up from the programming depends to a large extent on a person's choices. Some souls take many more lifetimes than others. Because you have free will, how you accomplish the soul's curriculum and how long it takes is up to you. Whatever your choice is, it will lead to learning, either sooner or later, so you can't get it wrong.

The light in all of this is that whenever you follow your Heart, you are aligned with the Whole, and since others are part of the Whole, following your Heart can't possibly be contrary to their soul's intentions. If following your Heart is the right experience for your growth (and it is), then whatever others experience as a result is also the right experience for their growth. What is right action for you must be right action for everyone else, no matter how it may seem to them. If they choose to hurt themselves with negative thoughts, that is their choice, but a better choice would be to let you do what you feel you need to do and wish you well.

Following your Heart is one way you can make a difference in the world. By being true to yourself, you become a model for others of a new way of living and being, and a catalyst for their growth. The beauty of this is that the more people who follow their Heart, the easier it becomes for others to follow theirs. This is how real change can come to your precious planet.

If no one ever followed their Heart, then growth wouldn't be possible. Taking care of other people's feelings and agreeing with their stories would be the primary value. This is, in fact, what the ego-driven lifestyle looks like: People do what they do because they *should*, not because it is right personally for them, not because it fits for them. This makes people miserable and leads to stagnation and entrenchment in egoic values. There is no freedom or joy in that. One's innate love for life becomes suppressed, and you are left with an unhappy and addicted society. Does that sound familiar?

There can be no growth without pain. Growth never comes easily in this world. But to not grow is even more painful and impedes the evolution of humanity. You see, your growth is not just about you. Your growth is also about the evolution of the Whole, which is evolving as a result of each person's growth.

When you stagnate, this evolution also stagnates. When societies become entrenched in egoic values, the evolution of the Whole is thwarted, delayed. Ultimately this isn't a problem, since the Whole has all of eternity to evolve. However, for this point in time on earth, this is a problem, when the survival of the human species depends on humanity's spiritual evolution, as it does now.

Entrenchment in egoic values is killing the planet or, more accurately, potentially killing off the human species. If this were to happen, it would be a great loss for the universe. You are a special and unique form of sentient life, and the entire evolution of the planet has been dedicated to giving birth to and nurturing you. And now you are destroying the very Mother who gives life to you.

This has to stop, and the only way it can is for each and every one of you reading this to wake up to your true nature. When you do, that will ensure that you become aligned with your destiny. For many of you, that destiny is related to saving humanity and the earth from further destruction. That may sound grandiose, but the way such a destiny looks is often very ordinary. Things change by each person making changes wherever he or she is, whether that's within a business, in education, in food production, or in some other area.

The planet can be saved by infusing every area of life with a higher consciousness. This infusion needs to happen in education, politics, the media, science, technology, business, agriculture, financial systems, and medicine, just to name some of the more important areas. Transformation in every area of society has to happen because we are talking about a transformation of fundamental values: from egoic values to ones aligned with life.

One of the most significant steps and lifestyle changes necessary for transforming society is to incorporate meditation into schools and people's daily lives. Transforming society begins with transforming consciousness because that's how values are changed. Nothing short of this will be sufficient. Meditation is the most effective tool for doing this.

When meditation becomes an accepted and ordinary way of life for a majority of people, your world will be completely different. Right now, to begin the transformation and turn the tide, much less than a majority practicing meditation will be sufficient. Fortunately, the effect of even one person meditating in a business, school, or other group can shift the energy in that area more than you may think.

Every person who meditates becomes more closely connected with other dimensional forces that begin to work through that person. This magnifies the person's efforts and influence exponentially. There is great power in one who is connected to greater powers than himself or herself. Those types of people have been changing the world throughout time. In fact, it is only such people who have ever made a positive difference in the world.

In times like these, which call for world change, many great souls come into bodies to bring this about. These individuals are able to connect with spiritual forces beyond them and receive the ideas, inspiration, and innovations needed to move society forward. Such times call forth help from other dimensions in the form of individuals who have a particular role to play in the transformation.

Another key change is providing a quality education to every human being on the planet. This is possible now with recent technological advances. Freedom and democracy can't flourish in the absence of an educated public. This goes for the United States as well. There is no reason for anyone in the richest country in the world not to have a quality education.

Without a quality educational system, a healthy political system is impossible. How can an uneducated and unenlightened public be expected to select worthy representatives? When education and consciousness change, political systems can change, which is crucial. Without the political will to set things right environmentally and in other ways, how can the needed changes come about?

Change has to begin with people becoming educated and raising their own consciousness through meditation and other spiritual practices. Since this type of change doesn't happen overnight, the younger generations will have to provide the basis for the needed societal changes. It's up to you, as adults, to see that today's children receive what they need to bring about this change and that they aren't simply indoctrinated into the same egoic values that are destroying the planet. The adults of tomorrow will need to live differently than most of today's adults. They will need to live like the hero.

Because the hero works in most of the same jobs as the ego-driven person, their lifestyles don't necessarily look that different, even though they are lived very differently. One of the biggest differences is the kinds of activities they are involved in outside of work. The hero's life is not likely to be packed with as many activities or the same ones as someone who is ego-driven.

Many of the activities the ego-driven person is involved in aren't part of the hero's lifestyle. To soothe its pain, the ego drives people toward pleasure-oriented activities or ones that just take up time, such as mindless television watching, gambling, pornography, drinking and doing drugs, sports, games, hobbies, shopping, eating, and going places.

Ego-driven people are entertained by these things simply because such activities take their mind off of themselves and their problems. Since the hero doesn't have problems nor does he wear himself down with thoughts about himself or negative emotions, there is no need for escapism or addictive behaviors.

In many people's lives, escapism, addiction, and emotional exhaustion take up considerable time and energy, which the hero puts to better use. If the hero has a hobby, it is a creative one or one that explores a particular interest and exercises his mind and ingenuity. The hero is curious and pursues interests, but the drive to do this comes from his deepest self and isn't a coping device for dissatisfaction and unhappiness.

The hero also has no need to be constantly busy, so his life isn't filled up with activity for activity's sake. The hero leaves plenty of space in his life for just being: for contemplation, meditation, creativity, resting, health, exercise, and meaningful relationships.

Another difference is that the pace of the hero's life is slower and less stressful. One way this is accomplished is through a minimal amount of multitasking. The hero, for the most part, does one thing at a time and enjoys it, while the ego-driven person juggles many tasks at once and is often in a hurry and stressed-out while doing them.

The internal state of the hero is very different from someone who is ego-driven, although they might be doing similar things, and this is a key difference. While many activities fall away when someone moves from the ego-driven lifestyle to one guided by the Heart, one of the biggest difference is *how* a person is in the midst of the activities that are part of everyone's life:

While the ego thinks about the next activity when doing something, the hero immerses himself in what he is doing.

While the ego does a number of things at once, the hero gives his best to one thing at a time.

While the ego hurries through the day, the hero slows down to experience each moment.

While the ego overlooks the beauty of this world, the hero drinks it in.

While the ego lives in a climate of dissatisfaction, the hero lives in gratitude.

While the ego lives mentally in the past and future, the hero lives in his body and senses, where there is only the experience of now.

While the ego pushes to do more, the hero knows when to stop and rest.

Perhaps what most distinguishes the two lifestyles is values: While the ego-driven person can't find time to do what nourishes the soul, the hero makes those things a priority. Because the hero and those who are ego-driven have different values, the world they create looks very different:

The ego values money and power, so the world the ego creates is focused on getting and having; while the hero values love and peace, so the world he creates is focused on giving, sharing, creating, learning, and growing.

The ego values the bottom line above human and environmental concerns, so it creates a world where corporations are not held accountable; while the hero values human needs and rights and creates a world where these are protected.

The ego values its own progress, so the world it creates is competitive; while the hero values the progress of all people, so the world he creates is based on equality, service, and cooperation.

The ego values having things, so it expends the earth's resources to get things; while the hero values the beauty and peace of nature, so he protects nature and its resources.

The ego values mental stimulation and pleasure, so it uses technology to feed addictions and fantasies and objectify and exploit others; while the hero values learning and growth, so it uses technology to help people share information, innovation, and understanding.

The ego values its opinions and prejudices, so it creates media to spread those opinions and prejudices; while the hero creates media to provide objective information and strengthen the democratic process.

The ego values its own children, so the ego creates schools especially for them; while the hero recognizes all children as his own and as society's most valuable resource, so he creates a world where all children are provided an education.

The ego puts its nation above all others, so it creates a world of nation-states; while the hero puts no nation above others, so he creates one world.

The current structures reflect the state of consciousness of most people on the planet. As consciousness changes, these structures will naturally change. Because many already share the values of the hero and long to live in a world more aligned with those values, a dramatic shift in consciousness is more possible than you may realize.

Once more people have seen through the programming, or at least begun to, this transformation can happen quite rapidly. It's not that difficult to see through the programming once its falseness has been pointed out. What most prevents people from breaking free from their conditioning is the fear of being different. But when the numbers of people who have seen through the programming increase sufficiently, nothing will be able to stop the momentum away from the egoic way of thinking and being.

This shift is being instigated by many in the older generation who have the wisdom to see the truth. However, real change will come when the young grow up seeing the truth about the programmed voice in their head before this programming can become more ingrained. Eventually the programming itself will change and become more positive and life-affirming, as people stop reinforcing old lies and stop inputing new ones into their own and their children's minds.

These are such important times, and those of us guiding the earth have every hope that this transformation of consciousness will happen in time to set in motion the much needed changes to your social systems. Your life is important because you have the power to become someone who can carry the light into the darkness. You, in fact, are the only one who can change your consciousness. It is your greatest gift to the world and your most important responsibility. Peace!

∞

If you enjoyed this book, we think you will especially enjoy these other books dictated to Gina Lake by Jesus: *The Jesus Trilogy* and *In the World but Not of It*.

ABOUT the AUTHOR

Gina Lake is a spiritual teacher and the author of numerous books about awakening to one's true nature, including *The Jesus Trilogy, In the World but Not of It, From Stress to Stillness, Trusting Life, Embracing the Now, Radical Happiness, Living in the Now, Ten Teachings for One World, Return to Essence, Choosing Love, Anatomy of Desire, Getting Free,* and *A Heroic Life.* She is also a gifted intuitive with a master's degree in counseling psychology and over twenty years' experience supporting people in their spiritual growth. Her website offers information about her books and courses, free e-books, book excerpts, a monthly newsletter, a blog, and audio and video recordings:

www.radicalhappiness.com

The Radical Happiness Online Course

Meditation will change your life because meditation changes your brain like nothing else can. Find out how. Get serious about waking up and becoming happier. The Radical Happiness online course will show you how and get you started. This 8-week course, which can be begun anytime, will provide you with a foundation for awakening and increase your happiness through spiritual practices, a structure for doing those practices, and support from an online forum. This course uses a combination of written text, instructional audios, guided meditations, inquiries, and exercises. The practices include four types of meditation, spiritual inquiry, breathing practices, a gratitude practice, love and forgiveness practices, prayer, and others. For more information, please visit:

www.radicalhappiness.com/courses

More Books by Gina Lake

Available in paperback, ebook, and audiobook formats.

Embracing the Now: Finding Peace and Happiness in What Is. The Now—this moment—is the true source of happiness and peace and the key to living a fulfilled and meaningful life. *Embracing the Now* is a collection of essays that can serve as daily reminders of the deepest truths. Full of clear insight and wisdom, *Embracing the Now* explains how the mind keeps us from being in the moment, how to move into the Now and stay there, and what living from the Now is like. It also explains how to overcome stumbling blocks to being in the Now, such as fears, doubts, misunderstandings, judgments, distrust of life, desires, and other conditioned ideas that are behind human suffering.

From Stress to Stillness: Tools for Inner Peace. Most stress is created by how we think about things. *From Stress to Stillness* will help you to examine what you are thinking and change your relationship to your thoughts so that they no longer result in stress. Drawing from the wisdom traditions, psychology, New Thought, and the author's own experience as a spiritual teacher and counselor, *From Stress to Stillness* offers many practices and suggestions that will lead to greater peace and equanimity, even in a busy and stress-filled world.

Radical Happiness: A Guide to Awakening provides the keys to experiencing the happiness that is ever-present and not dependent on circumstances. This happiness comes from realizing that who you think you are is not who you really are. *Radical Happiness* describes the nature of the egoic state of consciousness and how it interferes with happiness, what awakening and enlightenment are, and how to live in the world after awakening.

Choosing Love: Moving from Ego to Essence in Relationships. Having a truly meaningful relationship requires choosing love over your conditioning, that is, your ideas, fantasies, desires, images, and beliefs. *Choosing Love* describes how to move beyond conditioning, judgment, anger, romantic illusions, and differences to the experience of love and oneness with another. It explains how to drop into the core of your Being, where Oneness and love exist, and be with others from there.

Return to Essence: How to Be in the Flow and Fulfill Your Life's Purpose describes how to get into the flow and stay there and how to live life from there. Being in the flow and not being in the flow are two very different states. One is dominated by the ego-driven mind, which is the cause of suffering, while the other is the domain of Essence, the Divine within each of us. You are meant to live in the flow. The flow is the experience of Essence—your true self—as it lives life through you and fulfills its purpose for this life.

Anatomy of Desire: How to Be Happy Even When You Don't Get What You Want will help you discriminate between your Heart's desires and the ego's. It will help you be happy regardless of your desires and whether you are attaining them. So *Anatomy of Desire* is also about spiritual freedom, or liberation, which comes from following the Heart, our deepest desires, instead of the ego's desires. It is about becoming a lover of life rather than a desirer.

Getting Free: How to Move Beyond Conditioning and Be Happy. To a large extent, healing our conditioning involves changing our relationship to our mind and discovering who we really are. *Getting Free* will help you do that. It will also help you reprogram your mind; clear negative thoughts and self-images; use meditation, prayer, forgiveness, and gratitude; work with spiritual forces to assist healing and clear negativity; and heal entrenched issues from the past.

Living in the Now: How to Live as the Spiritual Being That You Are. The 99 essays in *Living in the Now* will help you realize your true nature and live as that. They answer many questions raised by the spiritual search and offer wisdom on subjects such as fear, anger, happiness, aging, boredom, desire, patience, forgiveness, acceptance, love, commitment, meditation, being present, emotions, trusting your Heart, and many other deep subjects. These essays will help you become more conscious, present, happy, loving, grateful, at peace, and fulfilled.

In the World but Not of It: New Teachings from Jesus on Embodying the Divine: From the Introduction, by Jesus: "What I have come to teach now is that you can embody love, as I did. You can become Christ within this human life and learn to embody all that is good within you. I came to show you the beauty of your own soul and what is possible as a human. I came to show you that it is possible to be both human and divine, to be love incarnate. You are equally both. You walk with one foot in the world of form and another in the Formless. This mysterious duality within your being is what this book is about." This book is another in a series of books dictated to Gina Lake by Jesus.

The Jesus Trilogy. In this trilogy by Jesus, are three jewels, each shining in its own way and illuminating the same truth: You are not only human but divine, and you are meant to flourish and love one another. In words that are for today, Jesus speaks intimately and directly to the reader of the secrets to peace, love, and happiness. He explains the deepest of all mysteries: who you are and how you can live as he taught long ago. The three books in *The Jesus Trilogy* were dictated to Gina Lake by Jesus and include *Choice and Will, Love and Surrender,* and *Beliefs, Emotions, and the Creation of Reality.*

For more information, please visit the "Books" page at

www.radicalhappiness.com

Made in the USA
Middletown, DE
12 July 2016